A PEOPLE PREPARED

A People Prepared

TERRY VIRGO

KINGSWAY PUBLICATIONS

EASTBOURNE

CONTENTS

· · · · · · · · · ·

I dedicate this book with love and gratitude to the members of the Church of Christ the King in Brighton, England and also to all my dear friends in churches from around the world who are in partnership with the New Frontiers International team.

May God help us to restore the church, make disciples, train leaders, plant churches and reach the nations.

PREFACE

In the face of a national crisis the President of the USA recently said 'If you take on an American, you take on the American people' – a noble statement underlining the strength of identity which being 'a people' should communicate.

God has a people and to belong to his people is the greatest wonder and privilege in the universe. God has always had a passion for his people. His ultimate goal is to dwell among them manifestly and to shout from his throne that they are his people and he is their God (Rev 21:3). His relationship with his people down through the ages has been the key and centre of history. Initially he brought them out from Egypt with the cry, 'Let my people go that they might worship me' (Ex 8:1).

The prophet Balaam who was hired to curse them found he could only bless! He was astounded as he looked at them and, instead of cursing them, proclaimed unparalleled blessing. He saw them as 'a people who live apart and do not consider themselves one of the nations ...' a people who 'rise like a lioness ...' invincible and with the 'shout of the king ... among them' (see Num 23 and 24). They were God's inheritance, his special treasure, but tragically they backslid.

For centuries they seemed asleep. Suddenly John the Baptist provided an alarm call for them. Appointed by God to 'make ready a people prepared for the Lord' (Lk 1:17) he was a herald of great things to come. Much more was to follow his ministry – a new dispensation of grace, the inauguration of the church, the beginning of the last days and the promise that God was taking from the nations a people for himself (see Acts 15:4). This 'international people' will ultimately provoke to jealousy his ancient people Israel, leading to a 'life from the dead' revival among the Jews which will bless the whole world (Rom 11:13–15). Israel, the natural branches, will be planted back into their own olive tree (Rom 11:24) and God's people be brought together in fulness. To that end Paul made much of his evangelistic ministry among the Gentiles (Rom 11:13) to win this people who were formerly not a people.

His strategy for the discipling of the nations was undoubtedly through Spirit-empowered evangelism and the planting of vibrant local churches. But how are we to proceed today when the landscape is littered with much that is called 'church' but is far from vibrant?

Praise God for the 'wake–up' call that many Christians around the world have been hearing recently. From Argentina to China, from Africa even to the slumbering churches of Europe, a new experience of the Holy Spirit is stirring believers.

Like most wake–up calls it is being greeted in a variety of ways. Some, troubled and unsettled, have not received it with much enthusiasm. Others are excited and freshly motivated with hope that a new day is dawning.

God has privileged us with a fresh opportunity to receive the Spirit. New wine is being given. We must have appropriate wineskins. Local church life must be restored.

We desperately need a rediscovery of the vital place of the local church in God's strategy, churches built on a revelation of God's grace, open to the ministry of apostles and prophets, filled with worship and prayer and enthusiastically committed to evangelism.

Such churches, reproducing after their own kind in a vigorous church planting programme, will play their part in the Great Commission to make disciples of all the nations.

In 1984 I wrote a book called *Restoration in the Church*. My publishers have often encouraged me to update it. In reality,

A People Prepared is essentially a new book in which only the chapter on apostles and some of the chapter on prayer resemble the material in the earlier book. The values remain the same but the vision keeps growing. Isaiah's words ring in my ears, 'It is too small a thing for you to be my servant to restore the tribes of Jacob and bring back those of Israel I have kept. I will also make you a light for the Gentiles, that you may bring my salvation to the ends of the earth' (Is 49:6).

Restoration is a means to an end. The nations must be reached. Jesus said, 'I have other sheep, which are not of this fold; I must bring them also' (Jn 10:16, NASB). The imperative of world mission must increasingly impact our lives and our agendas and motivate our actions. But we can only reproduce overseas what we have first proved at home. Jesus spoke of Jerusalem, Judea, Samaria and the ends of the earth – ever- increasing circles of a kingdom whose growth is guaranteed by God's promise (Is 9:7).

First we must change the expression of Christianity at home, then we can take it abroad to the waiting nations. Many of those 'waiting nations' are now ahead of us, of course. Western Christianity has much catching up to do. Free from the shackles of tradition, many churches in younger nations are enjoying unprecedented church growth.

I am convinced, however, that nations such as the UK, with its rich Christian heritage, have much to contribute to world evangelisation. The martyrs and pioneer missionaries who dignify our church history are worthy of a glorious posterity – a modern church, relevant and committed to reaching its own generation with the gospel of Christ.

As I offer this book to the Christian public it is my prayer that we shall see vast multitudes receiving the Spirit, restoring the church and reaching the nations to the glory of God.

Terry Virgo
November 1996

A NEW DAY

· · · · · · · · · · · ·

D urban, Cape Town, Miami, St Louis. The exhausting journey was nearly complete. Only two hours by car and I would be home, which at that time was Columbia, Missouri. My wife, Wendy, met the incoming flight and suggested an unexpected alternative. 'You must come to a meeting taking place at St Louis,' she urged. 'A South African evangelist has been taking meetings for a month, and dozens from the church have been attending. Some amazing things are happening!'

It was midday and I suggested that any morning meeting would be finished by now. She assured me that it would not, and sure enough, as we arrived at the crowded church building, we were just in time to hear Rodney Howard-Browne invite all the pastors to come to the front. There were about 2,000 people present, and hundreds went forward. Two large video screens clearly showed that some of my friends and co-elders were responding. When prayed for, they fell to the ground, as did hundreds of others. I had seen this sort of thing before on a smaller scale and so was not particularly impressed, but then I noticed something else taking place. Several people scattered round the building were laughing loudly and in a manner that seemed unusual for a church service. I thought it was rather strange.

At this point several friends noticed that I had arrived and warmly welcomed me back from South Africa. Happy to see me, they were obviously in a bright and enthusiastic frame of mind. Eventually, we left and completed the journey home.

On the following Sunday, after an excellent sermon on 'Suddenly from heaven' from my friend David Holden (who, together with his wife Liz, was visiting at this highly significant time), a number of people were invited to give testimony to what had been happening in their lives. To my surprise a man came forward immediately who had not been in a happy mood for some months. He had repeatedly indicated that he would probably leave the church and had seemed 'under a cloud' for ages. Mounting the platform, he amazed me by saying that on the previous Sunday morning he had been present and at the conclusion of the service Phil, the pastor, had invited the Holy Spirit to come. He then described how he had fallen to the ground and God had come to him powerfully. He concluded with warmth and enthusiasm, saying that he was sorry for his previous attitude and that he would be different from now on and be enthusiastically committed to the church. He was transformed. It was amazing – and it has lasted!

Next, a greatly respected church member and a teacher of Latin at the local public school told how she had similarly been overwhelmed by the Spirit on the previous Sunday and how she had fallen to the floor laughing. She had received a powerful longing to see her students converted and a fresh commission to give herself to witness and intercession. She was radiant. Recently she told me of the first converts beginning to come.

Thirdly, a very faithful church member, committed with her husband to the youth work of the church, told how on the previous Sunday she had fallen under the power of the Holy Spirit at the conclusion of the 8.30 morning service and had ultimately surfaced halfway through the second (10.30 am) service wondering where she was. She then related, in magnificent terms, how she had met with God in an awesome and almost fearful way which had rendered her unable to move physically for some time, but also how her marriage and relationship with her husband had been so enriched since the experience.

I was staggered at the outstanding quality of the testimonies and became aware that something new and wonderful was beginning to take place among us. The events of the following weeks continued to amaze me. A fresh and exciting dimension had entered our church life.

An amazing evening

Two weeks later a special weekend with a guest speaker was planned. On the Friday evening he spoke to a packed church and, on the Saturday morning, to an enthusiastic leaders' seminar. None of the recent phenomena had taken place, for which I was somewhat grateful since I did not know how my visiting friend would feel about such things. On the Saturday evening a packed church waited eagerly for more of his inspiring ministry. We had enjoyed an exhilarating time of worship; now it was time for him to speak.

He took the podium, opened his Bible, read a passage from Chronicles and began speaking to a hushed congregation. 'The story of Solomon is the most tragic in the whole Bible.' To everybody's amazement this sober introduction was greeted by uncontrolled guffaws of laughter from about thirty people. For five or ten minutes various attempts were made to continue, but the overwhelmed and overjoyed simply couldn't contain themselves. Finally, those who were being so affected were invited to come from their seats scattered around the congregation to stand together at the front where they might be prayed for.

The next thing that happened on this memorable night was that directly those invited arrived at the front of the church, they all, without anyone praying for them, fell to the floor, overwhelmed in paroxysms of joy and hilarious laughter. None of us had seen anything like it. The whole experience was totally unrehearsed and unsought. Several were trying to stop laughing, but could not. Others tried to stand up and were similarly unsuccessful. All hope of preaching was abandoned and gradually people began to lay hands on one another to pass on the extraordinary blessing that had so sovereignly invaded the evening. Many were still present at midnight. Several had to be carried home, quite incapable of walking unaided and apparently totally 'drunk'. This all took place in April and May of 1994. I left secular work for Christian ministry in 1963, but in over thirty years had never seen anything like it.

Back to England

The following week I flew to England for a previously arranged series of meetings. On my arrival I heard that Alan Preston, one of the elders of my home church in Brighton, had recently returned from the Airport Vineyard in Toronto, where extraordinary things were also happening. He had had a dramatic experience and had begun to pass on the blessing in the church.

My first meeting was a day with the elders. God broke in powerfully as we laid hands on one another. Several fell to the floor and prophecies of far-reaching significance began to flow. Next I had two days with a group of fifteen men who held senior responsibility in New Frontiers International. Leaders from India and Africa were present, in addition to the British leaders. David Holden and I began to relate what God had been doing with us in recent weeks. Almost immediately we were once again in the midst of an extraordinary outpouring of Holy Spirit joy, delight and in some cases drunkenness. Magnificent prophetic utterances began to flow. Our two days together brought deeper intensity, joy and anticipation. The following Sunday in Brighton saw further outpourings and amazing scenes of joy and excitement. Meanwhile, news was spreading fast among the churches that something was happening.

For several years the full-time elders in New Frontiers churches have gathered three times a year for two days of prayer and fasting. The following week about 250 men arrived at Stoneleigh – some totally ignorant that anything new was happening, others longing to hear the news first hand and have the opportunity to be prayed for. We had a time of praise, and then once again David and I told our stories. While I was still speaking, one man fell from his chair and lay on the floor; then another. Others began to show evidence of being similarly affected. We invited all to stand while we began to pray. Soon these 250 full-time ministers were in total disarray. Many had fallen to the ground. Others were laughing uncontrollably. Some were singing in a style normally associated with a drunken state. Normally on these occasions we pray for two hours, pause for one, and then pray for two, and so on throughout the two days. This time you could say that the programme became flexible! Again, extraordinary prophecies began to be given promising 'a monsoon of blessing' at the coming Stoneleigh Bible Week to take place ten weeks later at the same location, where there would be not 250 but 14,000 people.

Duncan Watkinson, who leads our work in India, described what true monsoon conditions were like and how the torrential rains would unavoidably dominate life throughout the monsoon season. We were filled with expectation. Another described a vision that he could see of someone who had recently laid concrete foundations, seeing the rains come and beginning to panic. He was rushing to cover them with tarpaulin for protection, lest they be washed away. But the word came strong and clear that there was no need for protection since we had been laying good foundations of doctrine and practice for years, and they were strong and secure and would stand well in the monsoon season that would certainly come upon us at the Bible week and beyond. Joy knew no bounds!

I asked the keyboard player whether he knew 'Singing in the Rain'. Praise God, he did! The familiar introductory chords broke out and 250 men began to dance and sing. Gene Kelly certainly never knew such joy and abandonment! Was this really 250 Englishmen?

'Taking the blessing'

After two days we returned to our homes and our churches scattered around the nation (and indeed nations). Duncan Watkinson stopped off at Dubai in the Gulf on his way back to India, where he gathered the churches with which we work to tell the story. Once again the Holy Spirit came in devastating power. A planned three-day stop had to be extended to two weeks. Then on to Bombay and Goa, where the same experiences followed. The pastor of the church in Bangalore was visiting Goa and in turn 'took the blessing' back with him to his amazed and rejoicing congregation. Simon Pettit returned to South Africa and, once again, the same glorious demonstration of the power and presence of the Holy Spirit followed in church after church.

Although I make no claim that this outpouring of the Holy Spirit can be called 'revival' it shares this characteristic associated with historic revivals, namely that it seems to be contagious. As Brian H. Edwards records in his excellent book on God's reviving work in the past,

> These spiritual awakenings were contagious and spread from one congregation to another. Often when a pastor and his parishioners heard about a revival in a nearby town or parish they went to see for themselves and frequently caught the flame and carried it back to their own vicinity ... During 1905 the pastor of Charlotte Chapel in Edinburgh visited Wales and when he related the story of God's great work in Wales to his own congregation a movement of the Spirit began there also. (Brian H. Edwards, *Revival*, Evangelical Press, 1990)

Soon we began to hear that similar things were happening all around the UK. Many churches from various denominations and groups were enjoying identical phenomena.

After two weeks, I returned to the United States where we had planned a leaders' conference. About 500 leaders attended from churches we serve there and once again God broke through in glorious ways. Prayer meetings and services repeatedly experienced these extraordinary phenomena and lives were being radically changed. The whole atmosphere of the church was being transformed. Morale, which had been low, was at an all-time high. New prayer meetings were started, services were extended and God turned our mourning into dancing. The church in Columbia, Missouri, where I was living, was totally transformed, as were others with whom we fellowship in the area. Pastors' conferences were arranged and many pastors began to press in to enjoy the blessing.

Stoneleigh '94 came around – an international Bible conference with 14,000 in attendance from thirty nations, camping in church groups in a vast agricultural showground. We were not disappointed. The power of God came flooding in. Literally thousands of stories can be told of lives touched and transformed, people saved, bodies healed, and people falling in love with God in a way that they had never known before. A year later 20,000 people from forty nations attended Stoneleigh '95 and, once again, God came in power. Every age group was affected including children who had powerful experiences with God and many teenagers who knew that God was setting them apart to serve him among the nations. On some evenings in the teenagers' meetings the programme was abandoned as young people gave themselves to deep intercession for God to send revival, and many offered themselves with tears to God, aware that he was calling them and thrilled at the privilege. Many leaders who were present said that it was the most awesome experience of their Christian lives. Now at our four-day prayer conferences for Christians in their 20s we are often overwhelmed by God's presence, as young believers pour out their hearts to God for revival and for the nations.

This is a new day, but what does it all mean? Where is it all leading us?

WHY RECEIVE
THE BLESSING?

hy have I so enthusiastically welcomed this fresh wave
of the Holy Spirit's presence? Many reasons can be given.
I have longed for a visitation of God's power for years.
Since I left secular work over thirty years ago, I have known a
growing longing for revival. I have devoured books on the subject
and set aside time specifically to ask God that I might see revival
in my lifetime.

The so-called 'charismatic movement' and the birth of
many new churches in the UK have certainly encouraged us.
God's presence has not been unknown, and we have enjoyed a
measure of blessing. But we have never seen revival; nor am I
calling this current move of the Holy Spirit revival, though the
spiritual climate has definitely changed.

For many believers who had almost settled for a faith
without feelings, this new outbreak has plunged them into a
glorious experience of God's personal presence. People have been
thrilled and delighted actually to feel God's power upon their
spirit and even their body! Their souls have longed for God and
now he is touching them in ways that are leaving them
overwhelmed and passionately in love with him. I have never
seen such radical changes in people who were previously formal
and indifferent in their churchgoing. Now they are so thrilled
with God, and particularly that he has come so near to them, that
their personal communion with Christ has been transformed.

Let Jane tell her story:

I've been a Martha for as long as I can remember. Let the Marys gaze at Jesus, but I had lots to do. I'm a pastor's wife, mother of two, part-time hospital social worker and have primary responsibility for our children's ministry. It's never been difficult to keep busy.

I've always loved worship in church, but haven't given it time on my own. My prayer life has been inconsistent – usually at its best when I was desperate. I didn't spend too much time with God as efficiency and productivity were important to me and that's where I got my sense of self-worth. I was very organised, methodical and even relentless in finishing a task. I structured my time with a plan or check-list and needed to gain a tangible reward at the end – a cheque, clean house, or completed project.

I'd known some Marys, but I couldn't relate to their romantic descriptions of Jesus and prayer. I felt relieved when other people received prophetic words about intercession and not me. I couldn't imagine being cooped up in a prayer closet. What would I do? What proof would I have that I'd accomplished anything?

Last year, our church began experiencing an outpouring of the Holy Spirit. I was dry and thirsty and tried to 'step into the river'. On several occasions I received prayer and fell to the floor. At first I received God's peace, but after a few minutes I'd feel anxious, worry that nothing was happening and get up. Despite this, I knew that lingering in God's presence was the answer. But how?

I was struggling with a sense of failure as well. I was disappointed with the way I lived for God, and I thought he was disappointed too. My past defeats were always before me. I couldn't sit in God's presence, but where else could I go? All my activity was making me very tired.

At this point my husband and I were given the opportunity to attend a pastors' conference at the Airport Christian Fellowship, Toronto. Usually I would have turned down the offer, citing my busy schedule or concern about leaving the children. This time I knew I had to lay everything aside and offer myself to God.

God met me in Toronto. He swept me off my feet and I trembled in his presence. On one occasion I was unable to rise for two hours. It overwhelmed me that God wanted me in his presence and physically kept me there. He assured me of his forgiveness, gave me a fresh start, banished my fears and released me to an intense and active loyalty and love.

Has my life changed? Well, my furniture hasn't been dusted many times, but the cobwebs in my heart are being swept away. I don't find it burdensome to pray any more. Nothing compares to God's presence. As I've started to gaze, seek and pray, he's answered my questions and calmed my fears.

God's great love has made me alive again. He's wooing me out of my fears and empowering me to work with him. To my amazement, I'm being stirred to intercede. Sometimes I know who or what I'm interceding for, but often I don't. Despite my past need for goals and tangible results, I'm now delighting in presenting my body as a living sacrifice. My desire is to be a vessel for God's glory. God has already answered many prayers and given me faith to pray for things that I wouldn't have before. I'm convinced that we will see the lame walk and the blind see, and that revival will sweep our city. To think I would have once settled for a clean house!

Unprecedented encounters

God has demonstrated his power to individual church members in a way that has been unprecedented to them. Ordinary church members (as if a member of Christ's redeemed body could ever be termed 'ordinary', but I will settle for the phrase at the moment), who personally had never actually felt the power of God before, are experiencing encounters with God's power that have shocked and even scared some. Finding that you literally cannot stand up because of an unseen force that is pinning you to the floor is at least unusual and is a simple demonstration of power very near at hand.

I used to read the testimonies of great heroes of church history and wonder what they were talking about when they used such expressions as 'wave after wave of liquid love' (Charles Finney), or cried, 'O God, stay your hand' (D. L. Moody). Now such phrases are not so hard to understand. Peter described the early church's experience as 'joy unspeakable and full of glory' (1 Pet 1:8, AV). Paul tells us that God's love has been poured into our hearts by the Holy Spirit (Rom 5:5). These are experiences to enjoy. His love is better than wine and now he is demonstrating the reality of that truth.

The intoxication that some have felt during this season of spiritual blessing has been extraordinary to witness. But Scripture at least hints of comparisons between the Spirit's fullness and drunkenness caused by wine: 'These men are not drunk, as you suppose ...' (Acts 2:15). I have known this verse for decades, but have never previously seen anything that required that kind of explanation. No church that I attended ever looked drunk before. Happy, yes – even excited and enthusiastic – but never drunk! Now I have seen situations of such delirious joy and delight caused not by alcohol, nor manufactured by religious hype, but simply through the powerful invasion of the Holy Spirit on godly, unsuspecting people. They had more joy than could be contained and the only explanation was God's overwhelming presence. John Piper has said, 'God's glory consists much in the fact that he is happy beyond our wildest imagination' (John Piper, *The Pleasures of God*, Multnomah, 1991). We should not be surprised that in his presence we can suddenly experience the fullness of it (Ps 16:11).

Some, of course, will find this difficult since their expectations of God and of Christian fellowship preclude the possibility of such explosions of delight. I will return to this subject later, but let it suffice at this point to quote the magnificent Dr Martyn Lloyd-Jones who said:

> The great and constant danger is that we should be content with something which is altogether less than that intended for us. ... In other words, certain people by nature are afraid of the supernatural, of the unusual, of disorder. You can be so afraid of disorder, so concerned about discipline and decorum and control, that you become guilty of what the Scripture calls 'quenching the Spirit'; and there is no question in my mind that there has been a great deal of this. (D. Martyn Lloyd-Jones, *Joy Unspeakable*, Kingsway Publications, 1984, pp. 16,18)

Significant contrasts exist between drunkenness caused by alcohol and Holy-Spirit-inspired joy. Drunkenness is usually sought as a means of escape – a step into unreality, a way to forget the pressures, sorrows and demands of life. Holy Spirit fullness, in contrast, provides not escapism, but the explosive enjoyment of a truth already known. For example, how do I know that God loves me? 'This is love: not that we loved God, but that he loved us' (1 Jn 4:10). Jesus loves me. This I know, for the Bible tells me so! But the Spirit's fullness provides deep assurance of that reality. God's love is actually poured out in our hearts experientially. Praise God for the Bible verse! Praise God also for the glorious experience!

Similarly, the Bible tells us plainly that God is our Father, but when the Holy Spirit floods the inner man, we cry, 'Abba, Father!' from a deep intuitive knowing which surpasses 'mere head knowledge'. Truth already known through Scripture is dynamically affirmed by the Holy Spirit. Again we can argue from Scripture that we know that we have everlasting life, but when we are flooded with the Holy Spirit's presence, we feel that we are already tasting of 'the powers of the age to come' (Heb 6:5, NASB). Overwhelming experiences of the Holy Spirit therefore do not provide mere escapism, but wonderful assurance of the reality of the things the Scripture testifies to.

Fiddling while Rome burns?

Some might argue that the world situation is too serious, too demanding for an emphasis on joy. The days are evil. We must make the most of the time! Can we afford to be thinking about such trivial distractions? There is a job to be done which demands all our concentration and effort!

Whereas this might sound good sense, it shows a lamentable misunderstanding of the great place of joy in God's provision for his people. Focusing on joy in treacherous days is not to be compared with fiddling while Rome burns. Nor is it to be seen as simply the cream on the cake – a delightful but unnecessary addition to something already perfectly nourishing in its own right.

The apostle Paul argued very differently. It is *because* the days are evil that he instructs the church to make the most of the time, by being filled with the Spirit, speaking to each other in psalms and hymns and spiritual songs, singing and making melody with their hearts to the Lord (Eph 5:16–20). God's answer to the lost and guilty world on the Day of Pentecost was to unleash on it a company of men who at first sight appeared to be a party of drunks! They were full of the Holy Spirit and joy, and the joy of the Lord was their strength.

Nehemiah was the first to disclose this secret. In his day, the people experienced constant hostility, many frustrations, daily drudgery, and even their own sense of failure, but Nehemiah put first things first. 'Do not grieve,' he commanded, 'for the joy of the Lord is your strength' (Neh 8:10).

Some of the church's greatest heroes have not only demonstrated steadfast and sacrificial obedience to Christ, but have also known the secret of making sure of drinking deeply of his love and presence. George Müller demonstrated his faith in God by caring for hundreds of orphans. He was no mere dreamer, but a man of action and compassion and tremendous responsibility. His testimony provides great insight:

> I saw more clearly than ever that the first great and primary business to which I ought to attend every day was to have my soul happy in the Lord. The first thing to be concerned about was not how much I must serve the Lord, how I might glorify the Lord; but how I might get my soul into a happy state, and how my inner man might be nourished. (Compiled by Fred Bergen, *Autobiography of George Müller*, J. Nisbet & Co, 1906, p. 152)

Let C. H. Spurgeon add his testimony:

> There are on earth certain Christians who inculcate gloom as a Christian's proper state. I will not judge them, but this I will say, that in evangelistic work they do nothing, and I do not wonder. 'Til snow in harvest ripens wheat, 'til darkness makes flowers blossom, 'til the salt sea yields clusters bursting with new wine, you will never find an unhappy religion promotive of the growth of the Kingdom of Christ. You must have joy in the Lord, brethren, if you are strong in the Lord, and strong for the Lord. (Robert Backhouse (ed.), *Spurgeon on Revival*, Kingsway Publications, 1996, p. 33)

What really thrills the local pastor is that these recent personal encounters with God have been followed by a new and sustained appetite for prayer and a new commitment to evangelism in the ranks of those who have been blessed. The Alpha course, for instance, provides an impressive example of widespread evangelistic activity closely identified with the Spirit's outpouring. Other excellent fruit include many who have restored broken relationships, rebuilt marriages and expressed their new overflowing joy and love in greatly enriched fellowship in their local church.

This new release of Holy Spirit energy is undoubtedly best nurtured in local churches which exemplify the characteristics of a new wineskin. The apostolic method in the New Testament was not simply to evangelise, but to establish New Covenant communities filled with God's presence and power and securely built on apostolic doctrine. The apostle Paul was never content merely to bring a message of explanation; he always anticipated that the power of God would be present as he preached, authenticating his message and establishing a context where spiritual power was resident and the presence of God could be felt. New Testament churches were filled with the Holy Spirit.

A Fresh Outpouring
in the Book of Acts

When selecting his material to write the book of Acts, Luke chose to give two chapters to record the extraordinary outpouring of the Holy Spirit that took place in Cornelius' home. He obviously felt that it was a spiritual breakthrough of great significance.

Also from our point of view the sheer number of spiritual phenomena makes the story noteworthy – angelic visitations, a trance, a vision, God's audible voice, and an outbreak of the Holy Spirit poured on people while they were still listening to the preaching.

Acts 10 and 11 mark a turning point in the history of the church. As God overflowed the banks of their previous experience, the early believers began to understand that the frontiers of their calling far exceeded the limitations they had set. I believe these chapters also provide helpful instruction for us as we grapple with the implications of the recent outpourings of the Spirit around the world.

Suddenly from heaven

The outpouring in Cornelius' household did not originate with a strategy meeting among the apostles. Peter himself was initially unwilling and the other apostles were questioning and critical. This was God's initiative, and it took the apostles by surprise.

Such surprises have continually taken place throughout history. The church has never grown in steady, predictable increments over the centuries. You cannot project a graph into the future and say, 'This is where we are now, so ultimately we will arrive here.' Church history can be understood only in the context of God's sovereignty and his chosen moments to outpour the Holy Spirit in revival. Iain Murray argues in his marvellous book *The Puritan Hope* that the Puritans held that 'the Kingdom of Christ would spread in triumph through powerful operations of the Holy Spirit poured out upon the church in revivals'. Church history has always had these flood times, – supernatural surges when God suddenly takes the field again, breaking in and altering history. In Acts 10 we have such an occasion. The church was steadily progressing when the Lord of glory suddenly said, 'It's time for the next phase – the great Gentile break out.' The initiative came from heaven.

Following his visit to Cornelius' house Peter returned to Jerusalem and was met by suspicion and some hostility. 'The circumcised believers criticised him and said, "You went into the house of uncircumcised men and ate with them"' (Acts 11:2–3). Peter had obeyed the Holy Spirit, but the brothers whom he loved and respected had not received his fresh revelation from God. As an apostle, Peter wanted to honour the leaders of the church and keep it united. He had no desire to start a splinter group within the church, yet God was clearly doing a new thing and he could not abandon it.

Human response is of crucial importance when God moves in a fresh way which clashes with previous experience. In Jerusalem the apostles could not understand why Peter had violated tradition and ministered among the Gentiles. However, because they remained flexible and open to the Spirit, they were able to adapt to this fresh flow from God. Tragically the church has often refused to adapt. At many junctures God has blown a fresh breath into his church through men like John Wesley or William Booth, yet they have been rejected and forced out of the main stream of their generation only to be honoured by orthodox evangelical Christians of later generations.

Supernatural phenomena

As I read through Acts 10 I am amazed at Peter and Cornelius' experience of the supernatural. Recalling the event Peter said, 'As I began to speak' (Acts 11:15). As a preacher he hardly felt that he had started when the Spirit powerfully interrupted him and overwhelmed his hearers. The outpouring was well beyond his control. God himself was pouring out his presence upon the church.

When Peter explained to the church in Jerusalem what had taken place in Joppa, his explanation was full of references to the supernatural. The early church was not stumbled by his story, but accepted it as a reasonable description of what had taken place.

Peter began and explained everything to them 'precisely as it had happened' (Acts 11:4). The phrasing reminds me of the introduction to Luke's Gospel, 'Since I myself have carefully investigated everything from the beginning, it seemed good also to me to write an orderly account for you, most excellent Theophilus, so that you may know the certainty of the things you have been taught' (Lk 1:3–4). Of course Luke goes on to relate strange and wonderful events – angelic choirs and messengers, a virgin and an old woman conceiving, a man struck dumb, and so on. Yet, having done his research, he sets it out in an orderly way for others to see.

Moving into the supernatural does not mean having to kiss our brains goodbye. New experiences may be outside our previous realm, but we should be able to articulate from Scripture the precedent and purpose for what is happening. On the Day of Pentecost, in the midst of that glorious first outpouring, Peter was first able to stand and declare, 'This is what was spoken by the prophet Joel' (Acts 2:16).

For those who have personally experienced recent manifestations, as strange and indescribable as they may seem, it is very important that we love others enough to explain as best we can what is happening. This type of outbreak invariably raises huge questions. It is not helpful to say, 'It is too wonderful to communicate; you just need to experience it and then you will know.' Peter explained very carefully. We owe it to our fellow Christians to explain any new experience in the Holy Spirit as fully as possible.

Sadly for some Christians any reference to the supernatural arouses suspicion. When I was at Bible college in the 1960s, on one evening Arthur Wallis addressed the students about revival. He illustrated his talk by referring to the revival that was then taking place in Indonesia and recounted stories of breath-taking miracles. The next day I was grieved to hear that the faculty were expressing concern about having such speakers. That evening I attended Westminster Chapel, where Dr Martyn Lloyd-Jones was preaching from the eighth chapter of Acts. He was at his glorious best as he preached on Philip in Samaria and the gospel with signs and wonders. I drank in his powerful words, thinking how similar they were to the message I had heard the previous night.

Afterwards I had the opportunity to speak to him and I related some of what Arthur Wallis had shared and the response with which it had been met. His reply was fascinating. First he asked me, 'How many points did I say that I had this evening?'

'Three,' I replied.

He continued, 'And how many points did I preach?'

I was rather unsettled by this unexpected questioning, but I could not remember his sermon including a second or third point. I replied, 'You only preached on one point.'

'That's right,' he said. Then he laughed, looked at some papers on his table and said, 'Those notes will do for next week. God came powerfully upon me while I was preaching.'

I explained my dilemma to him. I wanted to be biblical and respect the word of God with all its clear reference to the demonstrations of power, but was dismayed to find reluctance on the part of respected evangelical scholars to embrace any possibility of the supernatural today. I pointed out to him that he had that evening preached a message which embraced signs, wonders and miracles as he had preached with tremendous power about Philip's experience in Samaria.

The Doctor's reply was to point out that the greatest sin of the evangelical church is that we want to put God in a little box and tell him what he is and is not permitted to do. He encouraged me to remember the present continuous Greek tense and urged me to ask and go on asking, seek and go on seeking, knock and go on knocking. I will never forget his encouragements.

The confrontation with prejudice

News about Peter's visit reached Jerusalem before Peter did: 'The apostles and the brothers throughout Judea heard ...' (Acts 11:1). It is always a problem when news of you arrives before you do. How we would always like to go ahead and explain before other people have told our news for us! The Jewish believers were shocked that Peter had been eating with Gentiles and even baptising them.

The fact is that preconceived judgements are often rooted in a genuine fear of God. The apostles were not ungodly men; they genuinely wanted to do the will of God and keep the gospel pure. Preconceived judgements must not simply be despised. When the sheet came down from heaven and Peter was invited to kill and eat from it, he could not respond positively because he could not identify with the new phase that God was introducing. He feared God and wanted to obey what he understood to be the truth. His motives were pure. He wanted to obey God's laws against eating unclean meat.

At times of fresh demonstrations of God's power it pays everyone to remain in a humble attitude of openness of heart.

Prejudice accomplishes nothing, but the dismissal of those who raise questions is equally unproductive. Those with misgivings about new phenomena should not be dismissed as 'Pharisees'. Peter was willing to offer a humble explanation to his enquiring brothers, and because the apostles handled this new outbreak well, the church retained its unity and pressed on together.

Some have asked, since the sheet contained all sorts of animals, 'Why didn't Peter simply leave the unclean animals and take the clean ones?' Maybe the association of the two together made it hard for him to take any of them. This has often been a problem for Christians who find it easy to dismiss men or movements because of their association with others. Good men are often regarded as suspect because they shared a platform with others who are viewed with great suspicion.

Similarly it is possible to attend meetings where the power of God is wonderfully manifest, but other things are taking place which might be regarded as questionable. I have sometimes seen such mixtures and have winced at certain doctrinal references. In a move of this magnitude there are bound to be some mistakes. When we spot error we could respond as Peter did and refuse to partake, but I believe it is possible to lay hold of what is from God while abstaining from that which is unacceptable. Although the apostle Paul was well acquainted with the sin and failure of the Corinthian church, he did not deny that it was an authentic community of believers, and he even regarded it as the proof of his apostolic ministry! Failures must be corrected and immaturity must be addressed, but we need not deny the manifest power of the Holy Spirit simply because human trappings sometimes surround it. We shall always have this treasure in earthen vessels. I am so grateful to God that very early on in this current outpouring I witnessed greatly transformed lives. Having first-hand experience of excellent fruit helped me to overcome misgivings that I had with some strange aspects of what was taking place.

When Peter was invited to kill and eat the animals in the sheet he replied, 'Surely not, Lord!' (Acts 10:14). He had said similar words to Jesus when trying to rebuke him for predicting his death (Mt 16:22), but we are always on dangerous ground when we say 'no' to God. What he calls clean we must beware of judging and calling unclean.

J. I. Packer, who has so often served his contemporaries with such excellent advice, offers the following:

> We should be foolish to imagine that if God poured out his Spirit today we should be able straight away to recognise what was happening. Revival has always come in unexpected ways, through unexpected and often unwelcome people. We should not rule out the possibility that one day we shall ourselves stand non-plussed before an ebullient and uproarious spiritual movement, wondering whether it is of God, and finding ourselves strongly impelled by our instinctive distaste for its surface crudities and stupidities in theology, worship, and morals, to look no further, but write it off at once. (J. I. Packer, *Among God's Giants*, Kingsway, 1991, p. 429)

Is it you, Lord?

What Peter desperately needed to know was whether this new revelation was authentically from God or not. Peter's three years of training as a disciple had taught him that all that matters is doing the will of God. He had repeatedly been involved in unusual experiences. He had seen water turned into wine; he had been told to throw empty nets back into the sea having fished all night, with the assurance that he would now catch many fish. He had been told to hook a fish in order to supply his taxes. Like Mary he had to understand the key to life is, 'Whatever he says to you, do it.' All he needed to know was, 'Is it you, Lord?' One day he encountered the strangest phenomenon of all, namely Jesus walking on the lake. One might question the purpose of such a bizarre manifestation. What on earth could be accomplished by such an extraordinary display? Peter did not bother to raise very many questions. Only one sufficed, namely: 'Is it you, Lord? If it is you, bid me come to you.' If you love the Lord, surely that is all you need to know.

Earlier in the book of Acts Gamaliel, after seeing the apostles perform many signs and wonders, gave this advice to the Sanhedrin: 'Stay away from these men ... if this plan or action should be of men it will be overthrown ... if it is of God, you will not be able to overthrow them' (Acts 5:38–39, NASB). His advice sounds wise, but it was not. Rather than telling the Sanhedrin to stay away from these men he would have been wiser to tell them to research this very carefully as it would seem that an amazing miracle had taken place – a lame man was healed, disciples of Jesus were transformed and saying that he was alive from the dead and claiming he was the Messiah. Should they not have researched this with all their hearts?

Sadly the Pharisees were used to dismissing men without proper research. God could have arranged for Jesus to be called 'Jesus of Bethlehem', but he allowed the name 'Jesus of Nazareth' to stick, thereby concealing from their jaundiced eyes the place of birth that qualified him for messiahship. He allowed the Pharisees to walk in blindness as they kept their distance and applied inadequate research.

Peter overcame his own prejudices and baptised the Spirit-filled Gentiles of Cornelius' home. He was now identified, implicated, involved and in trouble!

THE GOSPEL IN WORD AND POWER

D o you remember the electric moment when you became a Christian? I can vividly remember the evening when I took that glorious step. I had never heard the phrase 'born again' before, but on that evening I not only heard about it, I experienced it.

There were many ingredients in the experience, but two were uppermost. First, I felt I was 'risking everything' on what I was being offered. I wholeheartedly put my trust in the great promises I was hearing for the first time of forgiveness of sins, eternal life and peace with God. At the same time I felt a strange sense of 'coming home' to God. I realised I had disobeyed his standards and needed to start again by acknowledging his authority and perfect right to expect me to live a different lifestyle – faith and obedience mingled together.

In Romans 1 Paul told his readers that he had received grace and apostleship, and went on to say that his ministry as an apostle had a clear focus, namely to bring about 'the obedience of faith among all the Gentiles' (Rom 1:5, NASB). As if to underline the point, he concluded his epistle with a similar quote: 'My gospel ... has been made known to all the nations, leading to obedience of faith' (Rom 16:25–26 NASB).

Clearly obedience and faith go together. In 1 John 3:23 we read: 'And this is his command: to believe in the name of his Son, Jesus Christ.' Why should we believe? God has commanded us to! John presses the point home with increasing force when he adds, 'Anyone who does not believe God has made him out to be a liar, because he has not believed the testimony God has given about his Son' (1 Jn 5:10).

One day Jesus was asked what work should be done by men who wanted to do 'the works of God'. He replied, 'This is the work of God, that you believe in Him whom He has sent' (Jn 6:29, NASB). God requires you to believe. This is 'the acceptable work' and that is why disobedience and unbelief go together.

Children of disobedience

Our problem is that we incline to disobedience. The Bible even calls us 'sons of disobedience' (Eph 2:2, NASB). From an early age our lives show the tendency to waywardness and disobedience. Our televisions and newspapers consistently report on a world in the grip of disobedience. If we all obeyed God, there would be no problems in society; but we don't. Children don't have to attend classes on 'how to be disobedient'. They manage it instinctively.

Disobedience entered the human experience at a very early stage. Genesis 1 tells us that man was given a glorious sphere of authority and responsibility. Made in God's image, he was to rule the planet as God's delegate. All creation was at his disposal and under his authority (Gen 1:28). One area of prohibition would test his true submission. He could eat of all the trees, including the tree of life, but the tree of knowledge of good and evil was forbidden. If he stayed under authority, he would have had authority – a timeless law.

Tragically the story tells of the tempter who challenged Eve to think for herself and question God's motivation. He insinuated that the Creator was holding out on the human race, knowing that they would be like gods if they ate of the tree of knowledge of good and evil. Why take God's word for it? They could know for themselves and make their own choices. They could be as gods. Eve made the terrible choice, swiftly followed by her rebellious husband. The fact is that God alone knows what is good for human beings and God alone knows what is not good for them. To enjoy the 'good' we must trust God and obey him. If we disobey we will have to decide for ourselves what is good and what is not good. While to modern men and women such a prospect may seem desirable, to the author of Genesis it was the worst fate that could have befallen humanity.

Man decided to act independently – to know for himself rather than to trust God. This is the root of man's problem. Obedience depended on faith that God is good, God knows best and God is for us. Satan urged man not to risk it and lied about the consequences.

Centuries later Paul described his apostolic ministry as bringing about 'the obedience of the Gentiles' (Rom 15:18, NASB). Nations locked in disobedience would be confronted with his call to return to God and to be 'obedient from the heart to that form of teaching' which he brought (Rom 6:17, NASB). Paul was incredibly effective in his task. He impacted great cities steeped in pagan cultures and established strong, outgoing churches. For example, the Thessalonians turned 'from idols to serve the living God' (1 Thess 1:9) as a result of his ministry. How did he enjoy such incredible success? When Paul wrote to the Thessalonians, he commended them for their faith and reminded them that his gospel had come to them not in word only, but in power and in the Holy Spirit (1 Thess 1:5).

Good news

To bring about the obedience of faith among modern heathen cultures, we need the same crucial ingredients in our message. Paul's method was not only 'words'. Words alone can be totally ineffective. As Eliza Doolittle cried out in total frustration, 'Words, words, words. I'm so sick of words ... Show me!' Modern people might well have the same problem with a gospel that is 'word only'. And yet I must point out that words are crucial.

How can obedient faith be established without a message being heard? In days of increased spiritual experience and manifestations of power, we must not turn our backs on the role of biblical doctrine.

The gospel comes in word. It is good news that has to be understood. You don't just catch Christianity like catching influenza; nor do you simply attend exciting meetings, hoping simply to get caught up in the euphoria. Philip's first question to the Ethiopian was not, 'Do you feel it?' but, 'Do you understand?' Jesus said that the unfruitful pathway in his parable represented those who did not understand the word. The Thessalonians, in contrast, received the word 'not as the word of men, but as it actually is, the word of God' (1 Thess 2:13). They understood it, believed it, respected it and found that it 'is at work in you who believe' (1 Thess 2:13).

So fundamental was the spread of the word in the New Testament church, that Luke described the growth of the church in these terms: '*The word of God* kept on spreading' (Acts 6:7, NASB); '*The word of the Lord* continued to grow and to be multiplied' (Acts 12:24, NASB); 'So *the word of the Lord* was growing mightily and prevailing' (Acts 19:20, NASB). Luke could have said that the churches multiplied, or the number of disciples grew, but on these occasions he spoke about the ever-increasing impact of the word of God. The whole world has been lied to and it is the church's responsibility to bring the truth to it.

The apostles regarded preaching as crucial. They filled Jerusalem with their doctrine. When forbidden to speak any more, they pleaded for boldness to open their mouths. When blessed with numerical success and the growing practical problems associated with that success, they insisted that others looked after practical matters. They were determined to give themselves to the word of God. Even after his resurrection, fully equipped with a body that could appear and disappear at will, Jesus did not overwhelm his disciples with supernatural tricks, but, opening the Scriptures, 'explained to them the things concerning

Himself'(Lk 24:27, NASB). This was consistent with his earlier ministry in which we read, 'He saw a great multitude, and He felt compassion for them because they were like sheep without a shepherd; and He began to teach them many things' (Mk 6:34, NASB).

Religious hunches

We can never jettison this emphasis, especially today when people are so full of their own ideas about God and life. Even when showing interest in the Christian message, many want to continue to eat of the tree of independent knowledge of good and evil instead of submitting their minds to what God has revealed in his word. J. I. Packer has said, 'People have got into the way of following private religious hunches rather than learning about God from his word.' Human perspectives of God and his requirements fall far short of God's revelation. 'You thought I was altogether like you,' God complains in Psalm 50:21. A. W. Pink said, 'The foundation of all true knowledge of God must be a clear mental apprehension of his perfections as revealed in Holy Scripture. An unknown God can neither be trusted, served, nor worshipped' (A. W. Pink, *The Attributes of God*, Baker Book House, 1975).

People not only come into the church with their own views of God, but sadly many within the church develop their own concepts by simply gathering up crumbs that fall from the wrong tables. So we hear such things as, 'I don't think of God like that,' or, 'My Jesus would never say that.'

We must never set the Spirit over against the word as though they were in competition. Although I have mentioned in an earlier chapter that one meeting was so overwhelmed by the power of God that it was impossible to preach, I am not by that arguing that this is the new evaluation of a good meeting. These experiences have been exceptional and we give great priority to biblical exposition as a foundation to all ministry.

Sadly some Christians have developed such a love and respect for the word itself that simply to hear it faithfully expounded can become an end in itself. Delighting in 'sitting under' good teaching, we can be in danger of becoming like Ezekiel's hearers; that is, those who love to hear a love song sung well, or an instrument played well. The fact is that Paul's gospel was with word and power. He reminded the Corinthians, 'My message and my preaching were not with wise and persuasive words, but with a demonstration of the Spirit's power, so that your faith might not rest on men's wisdom, but on God's power' (1 Cor 2:4–5). After Paul's ministry, supernatural power flooded the Corinthian church, and as B. B. Warfield has argued:

> There is no reason to believe that the infant congregation at Corinth was singular in this. The apostle does not write as if he were describing a marvellous state of affairs peculiar to that church ... We are justified in considering it characteristic of the apostolic churches that such miraculous gifts should be displayed in them. The exception would be not a church with, but a church without such gifts ... Everywhere the apostolic church was marked out as itself a gift from God by showing forth the possession of the Spirit in appropriate works of the Spirit – miracles of healing, miracles of power, miracles of knowledge whether in form of prophecy or the discerning of spirits, miracles of speech, whether of the gift of tongues or of their interpretation. The apostolic church was characteristically a miracle-working church. (B. B. Warfield, *Counterfeit Miracles*, Banner of Truth, pp 4–5)

Or as F. F. Bruce argues:

> The testimony of the New Testament writings to the regularity with which these phenomena accompanied the preaching and receiving of the gospel in the early apostolic

age is impressive in its range. The 'mighty works and wonders and signs' which marked the ministry of Jesus (Acts 2:22) continued to mark the ministry of the apostles from Pentecost onwards (Acts 2:43) ... Similarly the recipients of Peter's first epistle are reminded how the gospel was first preached to them in the power of 'the Holy Spirit sent forth from heaven' (1 Pet 1:12). (F. F. Bruce, 'Hebrews' *The New International Commentary of the New Testament*, Wm. B. Eerdmans Pub. Co., 1990)

Evidently the early church advanced through the preaching of the revealed word of God *and* through evidence of power in their midst. The advance of God's rule has always been through demonstrations of power. When Moses came out from Egypt leading the redeemed Israelites, power was demonstrated in signs and wonders and the opening of the Red Sea. When Canaan was inhabited, Jericho fell through the power of God, and other victories were won through the intervention of a God who acts. David advanced and he established his kingdom through God's powerful intervention. As in the Old Testament, so in the New Testament the early church expected manifestations of God in order that the gospel might advance effectively.

Gordon Fee has argued: 'The message of the gospel is truth accompanied by experienced reality ... God verified its truthfulness by a display of his own power through the ministry of the Holy Spirit' (Gordon Fee, *God's Empowering Presence*, Hendrickson Publishers Inc., 1994).

Truth and fire

It has been a source of great sadness to me to see two schools of thought within the evangelical church over many decades now. Those who come glorying in manifestations of power sometimes seem dismissive of those whom they regard as 'cold theologians'. I once heard a man speaking at a large conference saying that theology was the enemy of the church and that if only we could abandon doctrinal perspectives the church would be a happier place. What tragic nonsense!

We also see and hear those who love theological insight and savour the doctrines of Scripture expressing equally dismissive remarks about Christians who are enjoying God's power as though they were mere children preoccupied with experience. How I long for a recovery of true biblical Christianity where the apostle Paul, who wrote the book of Romans, also raised the dead! It seems that profound theology and great signs and wonders happily cohabited in Paul's life and ministry.

Jack Deere says, 'No text of Scripture says that the Bible was given to replace the need for the miraculous confirmation of the gospel message.' He adds, 'The miraculous phenomena were not simply signs of the Kingdom of God, they were an essential part of it. Miracles and the Kingdom of God are inseparably linked' (Jack Deere, *Surprised by the Power of the Spirit*, Kingsway, 1994).

Unlike free nations, in China it is nearly impossible for Christians to stand on the streets and openly proclaim Christ. The one exception is during the lunar new year season (Chinese new year) when the Christians send worship teams out to present 'cultural performances'. The singing of gospel songs is accompanied with tambourine playing, skits and dancing. Afterwards they present a gospel message and pray for the sick. Usually even the police officials, not wanting to spoil the festive holiday spirit, leave them alone.

> However, that was not the case in Zhoukou District of Henan, when a whole group of PSB officers suddenly drove up in their police cars. The head police officer stretched out his hand towards a group of preachers and commanded the other officers, shouting, 'Arrest them!' However, he immediately noticed that he could not move his arm and it became stiff in a stretched-out position. He

soon forgot the street meeting and returned to the police station. Many doctors were called, but no one had any idea what had caused his problem. Neither did they have any medication to heal him.

He was absolutely desperate when a PSB officer, who had previously read the Bible, told him, 'Sir, this is just like a Bible story which records how a wicked ruler by the name of Jeroboam spoke against a prophet of God.' He then read the Bible verse, 'And his hand, which he put forth against him, dried up, so that he could not pull it in again to him' (1 Kings 13:4).

The PSB chief cried out, 'What will I do?'

The other replied, 'You must find a Christian to pray for you.'

The police then very respectfully went to the preachers and begged them to come to the police station to pray for their boss, guaranteeing their safety if they did so. One of the evangelists thus spoke directly to this man who only hours previously had been determined to lock them up in prison. He told him to repent, which he did. Then the preacher prayed and God immediately healed his arm. He was so excited as he experienced this miracle of healing that he allowed the preacher to share his faith in the police station. Thus many officers repented and are now serving Jesus. (*Hong Kong and China Ministry Report*, August 1995)

Many cultures less sophisticated than ours in the West seem to have no difficulty in embracing the supernatural dimensions of the gospel. The amazing evangelistic success currently taking place in China, for example, is characterised by such signs and wonders as this recent report illustrates.

If we are to see a massive turning among the heathen so that they repent of their sin and reject their independence and embrace a life of the obedience of faith, we will need to see the same power and be submitted to the same apostolic doctrine as the apostle Paul brought to the nations so successfully. As a result of his clear declarations, he was able to establish churches of great clarity and authority, like that at Thessalonica from which the gospel sounded out to the whole region with powerful effects.

THE LOCAL CHURCH –
THE HOLY SPIRIT IN YOUR
NEIGHBOURHOOD

John was amazed. He had never seen anything like it. The sight drained his strength and he collapsed to the ground paralysed with fear and wonder. Then the most tender voice he had ever heard – strangely familiar it was – told him not to fear.

He looked again. None other than the glorified Christ stood before him; the one he had seen humiliated and crucified, now in glory that defied description. The King of the universe and the Lord of history had come to speak to John and to tell him a series of amazing secrets about the world and its ultimate destiny. Breathtaking visions were about to be revealed, with implications which stretched down through the centuries. But first Christ, the Master of all history, wanted to speak to some particular local churches about their present problems and pains, their joys and fears.

We tend to think that although Christ loves the worldwide church, local churches have no special place in his affection. But the book of Revelation shows Jesus not as one vaguely in the midst of the church, but walking among the individual lampstands. He knows each local church intimately. He commends one and warns another. He notes steadfastness here and apathy there. Each is an open book to him. His longing for a glorious bride is seen in his concern and ambition for each particular congregation.

'Christ loved the church and gave himself for her' (Eph 5:25). She is his special delight in all the universe. She is his joy, his preoccupation, his passion, his darling bride. In all creation one thing fills the heart of Christ – his beloved church.

We need to rediscover the incredible value and significance of the local church in God's plan and perspective. She is not to be ignored and despised; she is to be honoured and cherished. Each lampstand is not plastic but golden – of peerless worth to Christ.

Corporate identity

It is as though each local church has its own corporate identity – more than the sum total of its members. It can be addressed and described in terms that seem to imply corporate personality and responsibility. There are good churches and bad churches, strong and weak, zealous and lethargic. Some are even ripe for closure so that their members have to scatter and be added to other more healthy companies. Some are called to corporate repentance and rediscovery of their first love.

Christ is concerned with the life, health, ethos and atmosphere of every local church. He can prosper it and cause it to glow and burn brighter, or he can remove it completely (though we may keep our church doors open long after Jesus has removed the lampstand ...). So stop for a minute and think how much the Lord Jesus loves the church to which you belong. Ask yourself if your own attitude reflects his. Do you love your church or merely attend it? Christ's chief desire for each local church is to prosper it, display his glory there and set before it an open door of fruitful service which no one can close.

Individuals who have never experienced the joy and delight of belonging to a loving and vital Christian body have missed one of the thrills of the Christian life. Mere 'church-going' was never in God's plan for you. He wants you very closely knit with a group of dear friends with whom you can share your life. You are made with a need for close relationships. He does not want lonely Christians. He invites us to bear one another's burdens, pray for one another, confess our faults to one another, build one another up in our faith, encourage one another, provoke one another to love and good works. All this requires close fellowship, love and trust. Our lives need to be 'joined and held together' so that we can build one another up in love (Eph 4:16).

The love of Christ for us and our common love for him overflows into a delight in one another as we recognise each other as God's beloved children, so that each local church can become a manifestation of Zion, the joy of the whole earth. 'For the Lord has chosen Zion, he has desired it for his dwelling: "This is my resting place for ever and ever; here I will sit enthroned for I have desired it"' (Ps 132:13–14).

Each local church can know the full joy of being a dwelling place of God in the Spirit (Eph 2:22). What a wonder the local church is! What a mighty and glorious privilege to be part of one!

Satanic attack

We should not be surprised therefore that the devil attacks the local church in so many ways. He continually tries to attack relationships. He sows seeds of mistrust and distorts our perspectives of other people's failures. He tries to peel people off into loneliness.

By many varied means he tries to make people pull back from intimate involvement with a local body. He warns some that it is safer to keep their distance and just attend. He makes sure that others are offended and hurt so that they withdraw. He will use any and every weapon to drive people back into their own isolation so that they fail to draw upon the strength of corporate life.

In New Testament days the severest punishment that the apostle Paul would place upon a person was to put them outside the local church. Today, strangely and tragically, some freely choose to live in that dangerous position by their own volition, failing to realise what they are doing to themselves. Clinging to their fears or their grievances, they become vulnerable to satanic and worldly attack and are increasingly ineffective for gospel advance, which is ordained by God to take place through the local expression of the body of Christ.

Yes, the local church is not only Christ's delight, it is also his strategic base for our active, effective service. Modern Christians have almost entirely failed to grasp this master plan in God's economy for growth and world blessing. Many have given up on the local church by remaining essentially individualistic. Others have poured their energies into apparently more exciting Christian activities and organisations outside the local church context. But if they were to spend time assessing the lasting fruit of that choice, they might be bitterly disappointed with what they discover. If we do not earth our vision and zeal in the local church we will dissipate our energy and have virtually nothing to show for it.

A healthy church

The lasting fruits of costly mass evangelism cannot be compared with the fruits of a truly healthy church that is constantly involved in evangelism based on its own community life and outgoing family atmosphere. This of course begs the question: What does a really healthy church look like? What sort of community will experience the blessing of God's presence, and the love, joy, peace and growth that he supplies? It will be a church centred in heartfelt love for Christ. He will be the focus of its fellowship. Its existence will be for him and nothing less than him. Prayer, praise and worship will be at the heart of its corporate life. The teaching of his word will be fundamental because he has the words of eternal life and we love to hear him speaking to us. We expect to experience his presence in terms that genuinely meet our need of him and his love.

The church where Christ's presence is never felt is not a church worth attending. We are his people, his bride. We are for him – a dwelling place of God in the Spirit. If we exist for him, anything less than gathering to meet with him is a waste of time and a total failure to understand our identity.

It is possible for a church to function without that focus, where side issues can become central. Other worthwhile activities such as youth work, the Sunday school, the choir, the music, the community atmosphere or social involvement can be the foundation on which a local church is built. In the UK it is possible for a church to exist merely because it has existed for years, and people attend with little or no motivation at all. Against that background of frustration, many a zealous Christian who wants to reach his generation with the gospel will turn his back on the church to join an evangelising organisation. He will argue, 'Why work hard trying to evangelise my contemporaries if I know they will be turned off by my local church?' Gradually an unwritten law becomes apparent, namely that keen Christians will leave the church and go off to do something exciting for God. Also, finance is siphoned off to promote activities which fail to honour the centrality of the local church in God's strategy.

Some Christians are tempted to give only a basic minimum to their local church because they have become committed to releasing their money to other Christian work which they regard as more relevant to the advance of the gospel. They see the local church as merely ticking over and therefore not needing much income, while important outreach organisations obviously require a lot of finance and have a certain glamour attached to them.

A centre of activity

If these funds were channelled into local churches, we would see an end to the 'one man ministry', with all its limitations. More church-based evangelists, pastors, teachers, apostles, prophets and their support workers could be released, as well as other specialist ministries that could find their home within the local church and draw upon the skills of its membership. The whole atmosphere of the local church could be transformed, so that instead of just 'ticking over', it would become a vibrant, outgoing community.

Peter Wagner has argued that a church of about 100 members can easily afford two full-time leaders and that it should have three full time before it reaches 200 members. Where a small local church could not afford to employ a larger staff of leaders or release its own evangelists, it could work in fellowship with other local churches of similar vision. Within New Frontiers International we aim to see evangelists released to serve local churches in a region and leading Frontier Teams to help plant new churches. Everything is built out from the local church, with the goal of planting more local churches. A few years ago God spoke to us in prophecy telling us that we could accomplish more together than we could in isolation. Since then we have seen a number of corporate developments.

Many 'parachurch' organisations have come to birth through frustration. Perhaps such organisations dominate the Christian scene today because zealous believers who want to serve God on the front lines have grown weary of their own local church with its lack of vision or relevance to society. Although much parachurch work has been praiseworthy and motivated by zeal and compassion for particular areas of need in the world, the ongoing by-product is that the local church is then regarded as just a place for people who don't wish to get involved in the battle of winning the world.

Young people join the 'parachurch' organisations while others sit at home and send funds to help them. As the local church's best young people are creamed off, it becomes increasingly apparent that the local church is not a place to take seriously if you are zealous for God. These attitudes, whether conscious or unconscious, present a failure to comprehend God's will; namely the New Testament strategy of reaching the nations through church planting as the most effective form of evangelism. Paul, referring to the new Thessalonian church, wrote that he had no more reason to work in their area because the Lord's message rang out from them throughout the province and their faith in God had become known everywhere. He did not see the local church as irrelevant, but as a world-changing instrument in God's hand.

It is possible for many specialist ministries that have abandoned the church to function within a vigorous and successful local church. Then, those who are contacted with the gospel can be brought right into the family of God, rather than simply meeting a group of compassionate, zealous people. Businessmen's dinners and ladies' breakfasts are brilliant ways of reaching the unsaved, but why do such activities have to function in a way that seems to ignore the local church, when with vision and drive local churches could run similar events? Many local churches have lost their visionaries. Businessmen who are used to a vigorous secular lifestyle have grown weary of pedantic church programmes that are suspicious of creative new ideas. Such men endure the church, but their imaginative drive seems to have no place there. Some zealous Christians who have given up on their local church meet one another and find their fellowship only at the parachurch organisation networks. They give their chief energies to them and regard their local church as mainly irrelevant. New converts are added to these organisations and the cycle continues. It is easy to sympathise with this perspective based on frustration, but if the local church is coming alive again we must rethink for the future. For the local church to fulfil its true dynamic role, there must be a thorough reappraisal of strategy to restore local assemblies to their original calling and potential.

For instance, we must break the mould of the one-man-ministry mentality. The church at Antioch was led by prophets and teachers (plural) who were able to spend time in fasting and prayer and waiting on God together (Acts 13:1–2). Growing churches can afford to release more full-time workers who have in the past been forced to apply to other organisations if they wanted to serve God. Together they can form a strong spiritual leadership in a church, drawing the church membership into increasing spiritual activity.

Church-based evangelism

A new day has dawned for people called to be evangelists. They do not have to go away to join a specialist group. They can work out their call from the local church base and fulfil the Ephesians 4 word to equip the saints for the work of ministry so that they change the very atmosphere of the local church, avoiding introspection, but becoming a robust, outgoing army. There are currently about forty full-time church-based evangelists in the UK, working out from churches related to the New Frontiers International team, often training and leading the church membership out onto the streets with them into front-line evangelism.

The wonderful thing about the local church is that the people who reach out enthusiastically in evangelism are the same people who warmly receive the enquirers or recent converts into that loving community. They are not careless about those who have been affected by their outreach. A travelling itinerant evangelist is often saddened by the cold welcome his converts receive in the very church that invited him to come to evangelise.

A healthy local church is also full of believers who are totally committed to the lordship of Christ and seek his glory in the earth. They regard themselves as dead to this world and alive to God. They understand that this world is passing away and that they are strangers and aliens here. They belong to another society where friendships are rich, where righteousness is the norm and where Jesus is central. They are looking for his return.

They are conscious that they are pressing on to the end of this age. Although they will have a responsible attitude to God's creation, they will not be unduly alarmed that the ozone layer is developing holes. Didn't God say that this world would wear out like a garment (Is 51:6)? They are looking for a new heaven and a new earth in which righteousness dwells (2 Pet 3:13). Their hopes have not been built on material or secular foundations. Such Christians represent a radical alternative lifestyle and local churches are the context where this lifestyle should flourish.

Such people are not mere church-goers who have their roots firmly established in the world and its economic structures. As committed followers of Christ they realise that they have to live in this world, but take seriously the command of the apostle Paul that they are to live as though they had no dealings with it — it is secondary! First they seek the everlasting kingdom of God. The Bible says that we must work in order that we might eat, but man does not live by bread alone and life does not consist in the abundance of our possessions.

As communism has collapsed, the international community awaits an alternative to arise. Certainly Western capitalism is no solution. The church alone has the answer and that is best manifest through local companies of committed, excited, worshipping believers.

Like modern-day Daniels, most contemporary believers must spend the majority of their time working in a secular society. In their place of employment they represent the church's front-line troops. They should be exemplary in their industry, honesty, reliability and approachability, providing godliness for all to see on a daily basis. The church's witness in the neighbourhood takes place through them every day. As a lifelong civil servant, Daniel displayed a lifestyle beyond reproach. He was an efficient and loyal worker. He also lived with a prophetic perspective which transcended short-term career goals. His courage and clarity meant that he could handle both 'sacred and secular' to the glory of God.

Because they are clear about such things, church members will sometimes refuse promotions that involve family house moves, foregoing career prospects if these cut across church life. They are first committed to the church and the purposes of God. They do not have a double standard that says that missionaries turn their backs on the world while 'ordinary Christians' are not expected to do so.

The local church is the place where radical commitment to Christ is worked out. Once, while I was travelling in the USA, I met a Christian academic who had been studying under leading evangelical scholars in America. He had won a scholarship to continue his study in England at Oxford University. As a clear thinker and one who longed for people to discover the truth about Jesus, he gave himself to study. 'I thought that the world could be changed by ideas,' he told me, 'if only people could be exposed to the truth.'

One day, God met with him and showed him that ideas alone would never get the job done. God had ordained a method of displaying his glory in an unbelieving world. It is through the church, where flesh-and-blood people who have yielded their lives to King Jesus come together in covenant love, loyalty and righteousness, and are a light to the world, a city set on a hill which cannot be hidden.

King David had a great passion to build a house for God. He longed for a place where God's presence could be enjoyed and his glory could dwell. The city of God, containing the house of God, was his consuming vision.

Our goal should be similar. We should aim to build a house for God in our locality with the same devotion that David displayed. In our case it is not a material building, but a spiritual one made with living stones fitly framed together – a dwelling place of God in the Spirit (Eph 2:21, AV).

J. I. Packer has said, 'Something is wrong with professed Christians who do not identify with the church and love it and invest themselves in it'. (*A Passion for Faithfulness*, Crossway Books, 1995)

As Charles Colson argues in his book *The Body*:

Three or four years ago I came to the realisation that we had a scandalously low view of the church. The church is not incidental to the great cosmic struggle for the hearts and souls of modern men and women; it is the instrument God has chosen for that battle – a battle we are called to by virtue of our being members of His body.

That the church is held in such low esteem reflects not only the depths of our biblical ignorance, but the alarming extent to which we have succumbed to the excessive individualism of modern culture ... If we don't grasp this intrinsically corporate nature of Christianity embodied in the church, we are missing the very heart of Jesus' plan. (Charles Colson, *The Body*, Word UK)

Do you have zeal for the house of God? Do you believe in your local church? And are you giving to that local church the devotion which the Lord Jesus requires of you? He moves among the golden candlesticks, knowing them intimately and addressing them tenderly. He wants to bless your local church and to bless you as part of it.

ENJOYING GOD'S GRACE

W hat kind of church do you belong to? What gospel does it preach? The teaching you receive will very much affect the style of your church life. If you distort the message you will deform the church and render it unrecognisable. As John Stott has said, 'You cannot touch the gospel and leave the church untouched – because the church is created and lives by the gospel' (*The Message of Galatians*, from The Bible Speaks Today series, IVP, 1968, p. 23).

Before we look any more at the local church, we must address for a few chapters the fundamental foundation of grace on which this new community is built.

'Oh, you dear idiots!' That's how Paul addressed the Galatians when they started to drift away from the foundations he had laid in their church (Gal 3:1). They had started by rejoicing in the grace of God, but now they were reverting to law-keeping as the way of salvation. Paul was exasperated! He knew that unless they returned to the true gospel, it could only lead to the ultimate destruction of the church in that area. He was not content simply to regard it as a church that was developing with a 'slightly different emphasis'. He was amazed that his converts had deserted the grace of Christ for another gospel which was really a travesty of the gospel of Christ (Gal 1:7). 'You have heard me say it before and now I put it down in black and white – may anybody who preaches any other gospel than the one you have already heard be a damned soul!' (Gal 1:9). Make no mistake, legalism is another religion. It is not the gospel of Christ.

Walking backwards

Sadly many evangelical Christians know that the law cannot save them, but they insist that once you are saved you must return to the law to sanctify you and make you fully acceptable to God. This was precisely the problem that Paul faced in the Galatian church. The believers there had been saved by the grace of God through faith in Christ, but now they were being told that they must also be circumcised in order to be saved. They were reverting to their Jewish roots. The apostle Paul wrote to them, 'Your religion is beginning to be a matter of observing certain days or months or seasons or years. Frankly, you stagger me. How can you return to dead and sterile principles and consent to be under their power again?' (Gal 4:9–11).

At one time we were all under the power of the law. According to Romans 7 we were all married to it. The law was our husband – and a very fault-finding husband too! He always told us when we were wrong, but he never lifted a finger to help. He simply made us aware of all our shortcomings. Not only that, we could not argue with him because we knew that he was always right. He left us condemned.

If only ...

One day we saw someone we would far rather be married to – Jesus. He offered us love, forgiveness, mercy and grace to help in times of need. Tragically, we were already married to the law and could not have two husbands at the same time. Perhaps Mr Law would conveniently die! If he died then his legal claim over us would disappear (see Romans 7:3). But alarmingly Jesus told us, 'The law will never pass away!' Apparently we are permanently married to an overbearingly correct, fault-finding husband who makes us feel both wretched and rebellious. Is there no escape? Praise God there is an answer.

Although the law will never die (and will have permanent impact on sinners as we preach to them), the wonderful news for Christians is that 'the death of Christ on the cross has made you dead to the claims of the law. You are free to give yourselves in marriage to another, so to speak, to the one who was raised from the dead – that you may be productive for God' (Rom 7:4). Or as Paul put it to the misguided Galatians, 'Under the law I died and now I am dead to the law's commands so that I may live for God. As far as the law is concerned I may consider that I died on the cross with Christ' (Gal 2:19–20). Mr Law didn't die ... you did.

Now we are married to Jesus, we must never return to our old husband to be sanctified. That would be spiritual adultery. We have died to him. The great temptation among some Christians is to reduce Christian experience to the mere observance of external regulations. The problem is that the law cannot actually produce a godly life. In Galatians Paul argues that 'if a law had been given which was able to impart life, then righteousness would indeed have been based on law' (Gal 3:21, NASB). It is clear that it cannot. The law is an impotent husband. Laws cannot produce life; they only draw lines of right and wrong. Now we have been released and discharged from the law so that we may serve in newness of the Spirit and not in oldness of the letter (Rom 7:6).

His righteousness

Now that we have been delivered from our former overbearing husband, we are freed to enjoy a loving relationship with our new husband, the Lord Jesus. He does not just issue laws, but invites us to abide in him and let his words abide in us, so that we may bear much fruit. He is no impotent husband. He is full of life and freely imparts that life to us.

He also clothes us with his own righteousness as a gift. Paul tells us that God is willing to regard our faith as righteousness and on that basis he justifies the ungodly (Rom 4:5). He sees us as positively righteous – not just at the moment of our conversion, but as a permanent arrangement. Jesus Christ is our righteousness every day and he is the same yesterday, today and for ever.

Justification is a legal term borrowed from the law courts. It is the exact opposite of condemnation. 'To condemn' is to declare somebody guilty. 'To justify' is to declare him not guilty – in other words, innocent and righteous.

When you say, 'I feel condemned,' you are playing into the devil's hands and making yourself vulnerable to his accusations. He will trick you into trying to break free by increased endeavour. You must understand that the only answer is justification. You cannot be justified and condemned at the same time. If God has freely justified you, who is to condemn you? If God has declared you righteous, who can declare you guilty?

The devil tries to drive a gap between us and God by telling us that we are not clean enough to approach him. Now we need to 'put on the breastplate of righteousness', for 'I am not dependent upon any of the self-achieved righteousness of the law. God has given me that genuine righteousness which comes from faith in Christ' (Phil 3:9).

Train yourself

Discipline yourself to think like that. Refuse Satan's trick of trying to beguile you from the ground which you have in Christ to establish your own righteousness. As you do this day by day, you will learn to reign in life not through your performance, but because of your position in Christ; not by working, but by receiving the abundance of God's grace. Listen to Pam's testimony:

It's powerful stuff – grace! Strong enough to stand in. Always available, free and liberating. I love it. My middle name is Joy, but I would have excused you for prosecuting me under the Trades Descriptions Act during my early Christian life. It was a continual struggle to keep the law, and the inevitable failure produced guilt and condemnation. I became a real expert at those and felt doomed to a life of never quite making it. Depressing!

When I first heard about grace and freedom from law, I couldn't believe it. It was too good to be true, and I had to double check the facts. Then I realised that God accepted me totally, just as I was; that he loved me through and through; and that he gave me his righteousness instead of me having to try hard to produce my own. Guilt and condemnation went and I was able to relax and accept myself.

I have discovered that I can cope when I sin, and find forgiveness quickly. This has meant that I am a softer person, less critical and more tolerant of myself and others, and able to forgive easily. A nicer person. God's grace stops me writing myself off when I blunder, and makes me pick myself up, dust myself off, and start all over again. (What, not condemned to do time in purgatory first?!)

God has benefited too! I enjoy him so much! In fact we enjoy each other's company, and he's pleased with me. I worship him with an abandonment, revelling in his presence, whereas previously, to be honest, I was bored.

Life is busy, but I am no longer an uptight, self-righteous and miserable sort of person. (My husband says I no longer nag him.) I now own that name of Joy in reality.

Pam's testimony shows how God wants to lift the heads of his people through his grace. He never wants you condemned. The devil is the author of condemnation. Refuse him and beware every form of legalism.

Know the truth

Remember that the apostle Paul warns, 'It takes only a little leaven to affect the whole lump' (Gal 5:9). In this context he is not talking about sin, but about law. Paul saw that a little legalism could ruin the Galatian church.

What kind of church do you belong to? What part does legalism play there? Plant your feet firmly within the freedom that Christ has won for you and do not let yourself be caught again in the shackles of slavery (Gal 5:1).

Thank God for all the experiences of the Holy Spirit and for all helpful counsel from one another (although when the truth sets you free you are not constantly looking for experiences to free you or always seeking counsel or becoming dependent on others in a wrong sense). No mediator will need to come between the individual believer and his Lord, because he will be enjoying the intimacy of sonship and experiencing the promise of the New Covenant that 'each one shall know me from the least to the greatest of them' (Heb 8:11).

People who are genuinely freed from the bondage of legalism become highly motivated to share their new-found joy.

In conclusion, it is good to remember that whole churches that are built on the foundation of grace are different from those built on any other foundation. They become like Zion, the joy of the whole earth. No wonder people are very eager to be added to such companies and find that the joy of the Lord is their strength.

THE OLD HAS GONE,
THE NEW HAS COME

Have you caught your fingers in your mangle lately, or had problems parking your penny farthing? No? You are probably thinking, 'What is he talking about?' because mangles and penny farthings belong to another age. They are obsolete. According to my dictionary, 'obsolete' means 'passed out of use, no longer practised, current or accepted; discarded, by gone, out of date'. It is the word the writer to the Hebrew Christians selected when trying to explain the present status of the Old Covenant (Heb 8:13). Commenting on this verse, F. F. Bruce says, 'The very words a New Covenant antiquate the previous one ... the age of the law and prophets is past; the age of the Son is here and here to stay.' (F. F. Bruce, 'Hebrews', *The New International Commentary on the New Testament*, Wm. B. Eerdmans Pub. Co., 1990)

The early Jewish Christians had to turn from Old Covenant patterns and practices and devote themselves to the new and better covenant instituted by Jesus. For years they had related to God on the basis of a covenant grounded in laws, rules and regulations.

On Mount Sinai, God gave the Ten Commandments and made his holy standards plain. If the people kept the law he would accept them. They responded wholeheartedly, '"Everything the Lord has said we will do." ... Moses then took the blood, sprinkled it on the people and said, "This is the blood of the covenant that

the Lord has made with you in accordance with all these words"'
(Ex 24:3, 8). A covenant was settled.

'Do these things and you will live' was the arrangement.
But they did not 'do these things' and were disqualified. As Paul
put it centuries later, 'I found that the very commandment that
was intended to bring life actually brought death' (Rom 7:10).
Instead of qualifying him for heaven, the law condemned him to
hell. It highlighted his failures and judged his conscience. There
was nothing wrong with it – 'The law is holy, and the
commandment is holy, righteous and good' (Rom 7:12) – the
problem was with Paul; indeed, with all of us. Mere people cannot
keep the Old Covenant.

A new covenant

Centuries earlier, Jeremiah had acknowledged our problem and
promised that God would provide a new covenant. In the Upper
Room, Jesus used similar words to Moses on Sinai when he said,
'This cup is the New Covenant in my blood.' He scrapped the
old arrangement and gave a new one. While it was easy to
announce the arrival of the New Covenant, it is much harder to
get religious people – in Bible times and now – to abandon the
old one. Many pious individuals still cling to the mentality: 'Do
these things and you will live.'

Paul was constantly battling with those who wanted to
combine the old with the new. But it took time and effort to
establish New Covenant freedom. Only if Christians understood
their new liberty could they touch society, affect the pagan world
and bring the nations to Christ.

The covenants had some things in common (2 Cor 3).
In both cases God wrote his requirements down
supernaturally. On Sinai Moses brought two ordinary, flat,
blank stones to God. While men in other nations were
speculating about life, God was writing his holy law on
ordinary stone. The stones became precious and were kept in

the Ark of God. Why were they suddenly so special? Because God had written on them.

Paul tells us that in the New Covenant we have something even better: ordinary people undergo extraordinary spiritual surgery – God writes his law on our hearts. He supernaturally affects our lifestyle by changing our motivations and attitudes. We become disposed to doing good because we are enslaved to righteousness (Rom 6:18). We are also precious to God.

Although the same God does the writing in both covenants, in the Old Covenant he wrote on flat stones which remained external and lifeless, whereas in the New Covenant he writes on people's inner being. This spiritual communication imparts life. The Old Covenant came with a glory that radiated on the face of Moses and terrified the Israelites so much that he had to cover his face. But it was a glory that faded.

Paul said, 'If the ministry that condemns men is glorious, how much more glorious is the ministry that brings righteousness! For what was glorious has no glory now in comparison with the surpassing glory' (2 Cor 3:9–10). A bright moon might command the night sky, but it is barely visible when the sun rises.

Paul called the Old Covenant the ministry of death and condemnation; the letter that kills. In contrast he described the New Covenant as the ministry of the Spirit and righteousness, which gives life. You could hardly have greater contrasts: death or life, condemnation or righteousness, letter or spirit. Like oil and water, they don't mix!

The Old Covenant demanded a righteousness based on our fulfilment of the law; the New Covenant provides a righteousness based on our receiving grace. Through faith in Christ God gives us a righteousness that we could never obtain by our own efforts.

Justifying the ungodly

The scandal of the New Testament is that while we are still wicked, God is prepared to call us righteous, simply because we put all our trust in Christ (Rom 4:5). At that moment, he totally vindicates us in his sight and calls us new creatures. Then, because we are new creatures in a New Covenant relationship with him, he tells us to discard our old lifestyle and be consistent with the new person we have become.

Peter tells us that we have 'everything we need for life and godliness' and that we 'participate in the divine nature' (2 Pet 1:3–4). So God's promise through Jeremiah is fulfilled: 'I will put my law in their minds and write it on their hearts. I will be their God, and they will be my people ... they will all know me, from the least of them to the greatest' (Jer 31:33–34).

The New Covenant opens a new and living way to God. It replaces the locked-up system that existed in the Judaism of Jesus' day and which often prevails in some forms of Christianity today. Frequently believers are overwhelmed with condemnation and guilt, which stems from a law-keeping approach to God. Paul vigorously attacked the 'don't handle, don't taste, don't touch' message, stating plainly and provocatively that such 'man-made religion' had no value whatsoever (Col 2:21–22).

Jesus did not merely ignore religious externalism; he attacked legalism. He knew that 'to treat trifling things as serious matters, as matters of conscience, is degrading and demoralising' (A. B. Bruce, *The Training of the Twelve*, A. C. Armstrong & Son, 1894). Jesus accused his contemporaries of 'straining gnats and swallowing camels'. Preoccupied with little details of religious practice, they were overlooking the truly important issues of life. They tied themselves in knots and imposed the same legalisms on their followers. By training their disciples to have a sensitive conscience about things of no importance, they made them slaves to futility.

The story is told of a certain Rabbi Akiba, who, while he was imprisoned, was brought daily as much water as he needed for washing and drinking. On one occasion the keeper of the prison spilled half the water. When Akiba saw this, he said, 'Give me the water for my hands.' His brother rabbi replied, 'My master, you have not enough for drinking.' But Akiba answered, 'He who eats with unwashed hands perpetrates a crime that ought to be punished by death. Better for me to die of thirst than to transgress the traditions of my ancestors.'

We may have abandoned ceremonial hand-washing, but we have invented a few irrelevancies of our own. We must dispense with them, or we will produce the kind of half-breed religion that Paul opposed. 'Once we grasp the decisive nature of Christ's saving work,' writes Leon Morris, 'we see the irrelevance of all legalism.' (Leon Morris, *The Epistle to the Romans*, IVP, 1988)

If we transform matters of ceremony or tradition into matters of conscience, we sin against the gospel and present a distorted picture of the New Covenant message. We make God inaccessible to people and disqualify them because they do not know our religious practices. We should be helping them to face up to the big issues of sin and righteousness.

Sinners and saints alike need to break with an Old Covenant approach to God. Paul tells us that we have died to the law so we can be married to Christ and bear fruit for God (Rom 7:4). You will never bear fruit for God until you see yourself as dead to the law; never live a holy life until you accept your discharge papers; never enjoy New Covenant sonship until you abandon Old Covenant slavery.

FREE TO BE DISCIPLINED

The comment was in a letter from a friend in New Zealand. It read, 'Your messages to us on the grace of God have revolutionised many of our churches and our movement as a whole.' I was thrilled! Grace is wonderful. It sets you free to enjoy both God and everyday life.

Christ is our righteousness and he is the same yesterday, today and for ever. If you wake up in the morning feeling dreadful and have an awful day, Christ is still your spotless righteousness. It is impossible to establish a standard of your own based on the law. You have nothing to prove. Christ's perfect obedience has thoroughly justified you in God's sight. There's no more condemnation for you, so you can throw off any preoccupation with rules and regulations. You have ended your relationship with the law.

Sinners are still under the law (1 Tim 1:9–11), but it is obsolete for those who are righteous in Christ (Heb 8:13). You have died to it and have been discharged from its requirements (Rom 7:6). 'Christ is the end of the law ... for everyone who believes' (Rom 10:4). So be strengthened by grace and you stand firm in the freedom for which Christ has made you free!

Grace sets us free – free to drift, free to forget our Bible, free to sleep, free to dream. 'Aye, there's the rub,' as Hamlet would say. We can miss the point of grace. Wrongly applying it can make us lazy and motionless, as animated as a fridge-freezer!

By all means let us rejoice that we have been released from laws and the hectic perspiration that goes with self-justification. But if we turn our backs on everything that smacks of routine, we are likely to become disorganised slobs. Then, when someone attempts to develop disciplines in our lives, we will say, 'No legalism, thanks. Keep all that religion. I'm enjoying God's grace.'

Faith or fear

The vital distinction between legalism and discipline is this: discipline is motivated by faith, while legalism usually stems from fear and lack of self-worth. Legalism is a hectic attempt to justify ourselves before God, people and even our own conscience which is persistently bombarded by Satan's accusations. Legalism can bring some short-term satisfaction when we succeed in maintaining our routines, but the sense of fulfilment is fleeting. We become proud because we inevitably start comparing ourselves with others who have no stomach for such regulations. Remember the Pharisees with their ugly dismissive attitudes towards their contemporaries? Legalism preoccupies us with ourselves, not with Jesus. It leads us into bondage, and hands the devil the rope with which he will tie us up in knots.

Self-discipline has a totally different motivation. Paul said, 'His grace to me was not without effect. No, I worked harder than all of them' (1 Cor 15:10). Grace didn't slow Paul down; it stirred him up! It took away the dragging effect of condemnation and released him to run for God with all his strength. He even confessed to 'striving'. No, he hadn't missed the point. He struggled not in his own strength, but with the energy that God supplied (Col 1:29). Doubtless he sweated a lot, as did someone else who struggled in Gethsemane for us! It's wrong to think that grace produces a 'no sweat' mentality. Paul talked about running races and fighting fights; about dedicated athletes, hardworking farmers and committed soldiers. He was free to try anything, but would not be mastered by anything, so he 'beat [his] body' (1 Cor 9:27). That's discipline!

Sadly, grace can develop unhealthy associations. If you discover its releasing truth and marry it to that spurious doctrine called 'Let go and let God', you will end up in great frustration and fruitlessness. Some people think that Christians should abandon all effort because it leads only to spiritual bondage. They say that we should simply 'surrender our lives to God and let him do it all'. This is not New Testament Christianity. The Bible never tells us that to progress in the Christian life we must abandon our responsibility.

Certainly Paul exhorts us to present our bodies to God as living sacrifices, but he warns us not to be conformed to this world but to think with sober judgement (Rom 12:1–2). And he encourages us, among other things, to be diligent, fervent in spirit and devoted to prayer (vv. 11–12, NASB).

When you yield yourself to God, you are not passively 'handing everything over to him'. You are relinquishing your rights, sacrificing your independence. And this, Paul explains, is your reasonable response to the amazing price that Christ has paid for you. Passivity has no place in New Testament Christianity. Certainly you must abandon all attempts to justify yourself by striving to keep the law, because you will never prove your own worth before a holy God. But once you have found peace with him through faith, and release from guilt by his grace, you can throw all your energies into exploring the kingdom.

Baby and bath water

Some Christians embrace the theology of grace but then throw the baby out with the bath water. They insist that they no longer need a regular devotional time and dismiss its observance as mere legalism. A discovery of grace should free you from condemnation and guilt, but not from the practice of prayer.

Grace opens the way for deeper intimacy with God and more boldness in intercession. This is no time to give up disciplined prayer in the name of liberty. Moses was amazed that he had found grace in the sight of God, but he didn't regard that as a reason for abandoning prayer. Instead he argued, 'If I have found grace, let me see your glory.' It whetted his appetite for more!

Grace opens the door to intimacy with God, but unless you walk through it into his presence you will learn very little. Jesus sustained his intimate walk with his Father by giving top priority to disciplined prayer. He would not allow other people's expectations to force him to change his programme. Does your life with God reflect similar priorities? Having seen yourself under grace, have you stopped being a man or woman of prayer? If so, you are not a good disciple of Christ.

In the same way, God does not want to deliver you from regular Bible reading, only from a legalistic attitude to it. Jesus said, 'You will know the truth, and the truth will set you free' (Jn 8:32). Paul said that we overcome the devil's attacks by putting on the whole armour of God – much of which is to do with knowing doctrine (Eph 6:11). If we are ignorant, we are disarmed, which means that we are vulnerable to the devil and dependent on people to counsel us over matters which are clearly taught in the Bible. Some believers go through hours of counselling simply because they don't know what God's word says about their standing in Christ. They are 'freed' from reading the word, but don't know of their freedom through the word.

This can lead to a generation of dependent disciples who all think, 'I need release from this and that,' when God declares, 'You have already been delivered from it.' The less you study the word, the greater will be your dependence on specialist counsellors. Ultimately this could produce a church like that of the Middle Ages – no Bible, and a reliance on a 'priesthood'. Paul commended the Ephesians to God 'and to the word of his grace, which can build you up and give you an inheritance' (Acts 20:32).

God also calls us to exploits of faith, and faith grows as we develop our relationship with him. In the past, much private prayer may well have been legalistic, and corporate prayer unrelated to real life. But now God has shown us that we can freely come into his presence, and he has given us grace to be real with one another. We can therefore abandon unreality and externalism, and seek him with new simplicity.

Working with the Father

Jesus didn't say, 'My Father is working, so I don't have to.' Nor did he say, 'My Father is watching and I am working.' He said, 'My Father is working until now, and I Myself am working' (Jn 5:17, NASB). Father and Son were operating together. Jesus saw what the Father was doing and did it with him. As yet, few of us seem to be sufficiently aware of what the Father is doing to accomplish the mighty works that Jesus did.

Before you judge angels and govern nations, make sure that you are ruling yourself. Take your thoughts captive, discipline your body and temper, and stop wasting your life by frittering away time.

Once we understand our sonship and freedom from law, we will allow the Lord to call us into disciplines of faith, and follow the example of Paul who gloried in the free grace of God. How did he demonstrate that the grace shown to him was not in vain? By 'letting go and letting God'? No – by working 'harder than any of them' (1 Cor 15:10). It was not legalistic activity, but work inspired by the grace of God. He disciplined his mind and body while drawing upon that measureless grace which flows from the fullness of Christ (Jn 1:16). Legalism brings condemnation and bondage. Avoid it and rejoice in the grace of God, but make sure you embrace spiritual disciplines which will produce fruit to his glory and mark you out as his true disciple.

DELIVERED FROM A
CRUMBLING WORLD

On the day I was saved I laughed out loud when I was told that I should now have a daily 'quiet time'. What on earth was that? There was a whole new jargon to be learned. It was a new world to me. I had lived to the full in one world, and now I had to get immersed in another.

One of the new expressions I learned was that Christians should not be 'worldly'. This seemed to mean that there were various habits and places one had to give up. I duly got into line! After a battle I gave up smoking and drinking, and my beloved jazz records bit the dust. Amazingly, when I really got right with God, my cursing stopped overnight. I gradually started to speak the language of Zion with the best of them. Gradually my style of dress changed. I was no longer 'worldly'! But was I really free from the world? What does being delivered from this world mean, according to the Bible?

The world is part of God's glorious creation. Majestic in grandeur and breathtaking in beauty, it is also cursed! Man's sin brought God's curse on the earth. The beautiful rose now has thorns around it. But when the Bible speaks of the world, it is often referring to the spirit of the age rather than the physical matter which constitutes the globe.

This world system, in its godlessness and rebellion, is a force to be reckoned with. We are living on a rebel planet with only a little time left. How are we to live in this spherical time bomb as its fuse burns shorter? Living on the edge of time requires great wisdom. We dare not drift into the carelessness that characterised the earth when God sent the flood.

You don't belong

The first thing to grasp is that if you are a disciple of the Lord Jesus you don't really belong here. You are not of the world, just as he was not. Jesus was doubtless the world's best teacher, but the world did not produce him. He came from above. He was a stranger here, and when you became a Christian that also became true of you. You have been born from above. Your citizenship is in heaven. Your new life did not originate in your natural flesh. Your neighbour may think you belong to this world but God says you do not. The world does not know you because it did not know him (1 Jn 3:1). Our Lord's human brothers did not believe that he was not of this world, but those who saw him transfigured and shining on the Mount knew differently. Don't rush over this truth. If you really believe it, it will change your whole lifestyle. Abraham had far less revelation when he uprooted and left Ur of the Chaldeans looking for the city of God.

You cannot escape the world by avoiding certain places designated 'worldly'. The whole world lies in the evil one, not just the seedy downtown areas. Nor is it God's purpose that you retire to some mediaeval monastery or even a twentieth-century charismatic commune. Jesus prayed that you should not be taken out of the world (Jn 17:15). You are needed there as salt and light. The church of Christ is like a lily among the thorns, not an orchid in the greenhouse.

Down through the ages godly men and women have had to come to terms with this dilemma. How do the righteous live in an unrighteous world? How do you overcome the dangers of worldliness? Many have found a very simple answer. They have short-listed a number of places and habits and said that if you avoid them you are not worldly. As the old ditty has it: 'I don't smoke, I don't chew, I don't mix with those who do!' Tragically, the evangelical world has often settled for such a stance, with slight adjustments depending on what your denominational traditions and national culture consider is taboo. But this is no answer at all.

In daily life you are released from the world not by a rule book, but by a relationship. Rather than issuing young Timothy with a catalogue of what was 'kosher', Paul gave him a principle for living which looks very dangerous indeed. He said, 'Everything God created is good, and nothing is to be rejected if it is received with thanksgiving, because it is consecrated by the word of God and prayer' (1 Tim 4:4). In other words, if you can genuinely thank God for it, it is good.

A good conscience

As Paul argues in Colossians 3, you are to let the peace of God rule in your heart and always obey your conscience. One man's conscience may allow what another's may refuse, but you must not impose either your liberty or your law on another. Rather, the conscience must be continually educated and adjusted by the Scriptures. You must never do something your conscience rejects just because another Christian has liberty to indulge in it.

'One man has faith that he may eat all things, but he who is weak eats vegetables only. One man regards one day above another, another regards every day alike. Let each man be fully convinced in his own mind' (Rom 14:2, 5, NASB). In the matter of food, drink, days and so on, there will be a variety of interpretations as to what is worldly. Your peaceful relationship with your heavenly Father is the New Testament plumbline. 'He who doubts is condemned if he eats because his eating is not from faith; and whatever is not from faith is sin' (Rom 14:23, NASB). In judging worldliness, as in every other area of spiritual life, the letter kills, but the spirit gives life.

Friendship with this world is enmity with God, yet Jesus was a friend of sinners. How do you hold the balance? Not by rules and regulations, but by a deep change of heart. In Colossians Paul argues, 'Since you died with Christ to the basic principles of this world, why, as though you still belonged to it, do you submit to its rules: "Do not handle! Do not taste! Do not touch!"? ... they are based on human commands and teachings' (2:20–22).These things, he argues, have an appearance of wisdom in self-made religion or 'delight in religiousness' (Col 3:23, NASB margin), but are of no real value. You may delight in little rules about things Christians should not do, but if you think this is avoiding worldliness you are sadly mistaken.

What did Jesus say about worldliness? He didn't seem to get involved in the 'short-list' approach. He was far more radical and clear cut.

Two masters

Where does the real power of the world lie? Jesus made it plain that good seed could be totally choked by the cares of the world and the deceitfulness of riches. 'You cannot serve two masters,' he proclaimed. 'You cannot serve God and money.' A man can easily avoid the forbidden short-list but be totally worldly, because worldly cares and riches hold him in their vice-like grip. He is as ambitious as any worldly man. He makes major decisions regarding career and home location in the same way as his unbelieving work colleague. He is essentially serving mammon with a religious façade. Promotion which requires a house move is a fact of life in our present society. How Christians respond to this challenge shows whether or not they are worldly. Which comes first – the kingdom of God or career prospects?

You may be horrified at the suggestion that you are in the grip of the world when you choose career first, but many have thrown away Christian fellowship and godly ministry by moving into a spiritual wilderness for a career promotion. The price of such a move can prove to be very high – like Esau, giving up your inheritance for a mess of pottage. Jesus said more about money than most other matters, so beware the deceitfulness of riches. Jesus said, 'Where your treasure is, there will your heart be also.'

The world has a built-in decay factor of 'rust' and 'moth' which is meant to wean you from this passing age. Jesus undoubtedly wants you to be seriously committed to giving away money. You can't take it with you but you can send it on ahead! Get your heart and mind set on the world to come. Jesus calls you to take up your cross and follow him, and lay down your life in this world. He who hates his life in this world will find it. When Paul spoke of glorying in the cross of Christ, he was not simply conjuring up the memory of the crucifixion. Rather, he gloried in the cross through which he had been crucified to the world and the world to him (Gal 6:14). The world no longer lured him. Formerly, his hopes and training had pointed him to a successful career as a leading Pharisee. Now he regarded that as utter rubbish. Even the religious world held no attraction for him.

Jesus suffered 'outside the camp' for our sakes and we are invited to join him there (Heb 13:12–14). It is hard to be outside the camp – to be the odd one out at work, school or college. You are often sorely tempted to come back inside by conforming to the world's wisdom. From the beginning man has been tempted to gain wisdom without God. The fruit of the tree of knowledge was to make one wise and Eve was keen to have it.

Worldly wisdom

Independent wisdom is the proof of worldliness, according to the Bible. God has provided a way of salvation that cuts right across it. His gospel is foolishness to the worldly man. If a man regards himself wise in this world, he must become foolish in order to become truly wise (1 Cor 3:18). He has to become like a little child and humble himself. Hence, in the kingdom of God there are not many wise according to human standards. Christ crucified is foolishness to the world's mind. The worldly man, in his pride, loves to have his own opinion about a matter, but the mark of a true believer is that his mouth has been closed by God (Rom 3:19). God does not require your opinion.

The Lord knows the reasonings of the wise – that they are useless (1 Cor 3:20). If you for ever explain away the creation story, the Virgin birth and Bible miracles, you simply yield to worldly wisdom and say that modern man really knows best. By faith I understand the world was created by the word of God. I shall never arrive at that conclusion through worldly science; only by submitting in faith to God's word.

The man of the world loves to mock the believer by ridiculing Scripture's account of creation, but the Bible has always been foolishness to the world, and always will be. Some theologians try to bridge the gap by retaining portions of Christian teaching, while rejecting what is unacceptable to the world's current thinking. They have a hopeless task. They will never win the world; the world has already won them.

As R. T. Kendall argues, 'It is not our task to destigmatise the faith ... but rather to bear the stigma as we bear the cross of Jesus. We must be willing to be unvindicated and laughed at, and not rush to make our belief in the Bible credible to others.' Pointing out that Hebrews 11:3 tells us that it is by faith that we understand that the universe was created from nothing, he adds,

> Many scientists may not understand. But 'we' do – we who are the family of God. Because creation really is a family secret. It is something we understand by faith ... The Christian should never apologise for what has been revealed by the Holy Spirit, regardless of whether those outside the family ever come to affirm the same thing. (R. T. Kendall, *Who By Faith*, Hodder and Stoughton, 1981)

Paul, a brilliant young man fully trained at Gamaliel's school, was willing to be mocked by fellow academics of his day by preaching the foolishness of the cross. He gloried in the cross which set him free from the crumbling world, its standards and its wisdom. He realised that building life for this world alone is short-sighted. Live in the world we must, but we know its time is running out. It simply makes no sense to put all your trust in something with no permanence. 'Let those who deal with this world be as though they had no dealings with it, for the form of this world is passing away' (1 Cor 7:31). You have to work in order to eat, but don't put your roots down too deeply. 'The darkness is passing and the true light is already shining' (1 Jn 2:8). John pictures a long night.

It is passing away

Darkness invaded God's glorious creation, and the world became a place of spiritual gloom, but eternal dawn is breaking. Paul had a similar vision in Romans 13:12 where he said, 'The night is nearly over; the day is almost here.' God's glorious eternal day is about to break through the darkness. Time is running out. It is nearly time for a new heaven and a new earth.

I recall flying home through the night after one overseas trip and arriving in London in the very early morning. As we flew over southern England the sky was black. Then I suddenly saw what looked like a thin golden line along the horizon. Gradually the line broadened and filled with beautiful colours – mixtures of gold, yellow and orange. The sky above it gradually became a beautiful deep blue instead of black.

All the passengers were staring at this beautiful sight. Then we began to descend into the clouds and quickly landed. On the ground it was still pitch black, but above the clouds we had seen dawn breaking on the horizon. We knew, despite the fact that it was still hidden by the clouds, that 'the night is nearly over'.

Look out! This age is about to pass away. We are living on the edge of time. 'Set your minds on things above, not on earthly things. When Christ, who is your life, appears, then you also will appear with him in glory' (Col 3:2, 4). 'When he appears, we shall be like him, for we shall see him as he is' (1 Jn 3:2). Live in the light of the eternal day that is about to break and be free from the power of this crumbling world.

When Peter preached his Pentecost sermon it included a call to escape that perverse generation (Acts 2:40). He invited them to leave one world and join another. Those who responded through faith and baptism were 'added' to the new community of King Jesus. They joined the church. This, of course, did not mean that on Sundays they began to attend the rather outdated building on the corner! They embraced a community with a totally different lifestyle, whose lives were intimately interwoven and where the presence of God's Spirit was continually enjoyed. The church, God's alternative society, had begun.

THE STRATEGIC
LOCAL CHURCH

A t one time, 'church planting' was almost a dirty word in the UK. Why did we need new churches? St Whatever's had been there for centuries and plenty of Baptist, Methodist, URC and other churches dotted the landscape. Why bother with more?

Now we are in a new era and such fresh initiatives as Dawn 2000 have changed people's thinking. Church planting has become a far more acceptable concept. Local churches are undoubtedly the strategic key for world evangelisation. The early apostles committed themselves not only to evangelism, but also to a clear church-planting programme.

A properly functioning local church should provide a base for Christian community and witness. We praise God for every form of evangelism and every effort made to make Jesus known. But our instructions are to make disciples of every nation and the local church is the best possible setting for discipleship. Paul was never content to see people simply become Christians; he wanted a local church established. So he would return to every town he had visited to make sure that elders were in place and that church life could function properly. Only then was he content that the area had been effectively evangelised.

When the apostles in Jerusalem heard that great evangelistic breakthroughs had occurred in Samaria and Antioch, they were quick to investigate. They would not have been content merely to hear that hundreds of converts had responded to the isolated evangelist's ministry – however amazing the miracles. They were not looking for crowds of new converts, but for churches of new disciples. Unless they saw churches which were being founded on apostolic doctrine, they would not be fulfilling the Great Commission.

If that was the biblical method, what were biblical churches like? Since the early church was born in the fires of persecution, much church life would have been in secret. There was surely an intimate house-church style with room for outward diversity. So what were the essentials which we must build into our churches today?

A body of believers

First, they were a body of believers. Early Christianity knew nothing of a mixture of saved and unsaved practising a social phenomenon called 'church-going'. Addition to the New Testament church implied submission to Christ. This was expressed in believers' baptism – a non-negotiable requirement which Jesus had laid down. No Bible-believing preacher is free to offer salvation and church membership without following this essential command. When believers are baptised, they demonstrate that they have died to one lifestyle and been raised into a new one where Jesus Christ is Lord. They are joining the community of the King. They are then introduced to a family of believers. For some early Christians, joining the church would have meant being disowned by their Jewish or pagan relations. The church really did become their family. A biblical church is a community of rich relationships. Christian brothers and sisters will become closer than any blood relations.

Building biblically implies building intimately. We are not mere 'meeting attenders'. We are a fellowship of disciples who share our lives. The word *koinonia*, often translated 'fellowship' in the New Testament, suggests partnership. Peter, James and John were fishermen 'partners' (same root Greek word). If one of them had a torn net, the others would rush to his aid. Partnership implies shared responsibility and shared rewards.

The root of sinfulness is independence – everyone turning to his own way (Is 53:6) and doing what is right in his own eyes (Judg 21:25). The church is God's antidote to independence. It gives you the opportunity to open up to others, with all the pains and pleasures which accompany that process. The moment you believe in Christ you are saved and thoroughly justified in God's sight. But from that time a process of sanctification begins to take place. You were a sinner; now God wants to make you holy. You had huge areas of selfishness, thoughtlessness, pride, fear, anger and so on. Many of these things can be overcome by personal application of the truth of God's word and the inner work of the Holy Spirit. But much of your character will change only through close fellowship with other Christians and discipleship accountability. Jesus discipled twelve men. Their experiences included wonderful encouragements: 'Blessed are you, Simon, son of Jonah!' and fearful confrontations: 'You are thinking from men's point of view, not God's.' Impetuous Simon was discipled and became Peter, the Rock.

Biblical churches discourage 'hiding in the crowd' and promote the need to be discipled – in character, in gifting and in spheres of service.

Making disciples

Jesus gave the agenda to the church in the Great Commission: 'Go and make disciples of all nations' (Mt 28:19). Disciple-making is the foundation for church life. A church is a body of disciples. If a church has no disciple-making activity we must question whether it is a biblical church. If there is no disciple-making going on in your church, you need to do something about it. Christians are born, but disciples are made. We are commanded to make disciples, not bully people into submission, but lovingly encouraging them into wholeness and meaningful relationships. Paul wanted to present every person mature (Col 1:18) and was sad when he had to address Christians of years' standing as 'babes in Christ'. He knew they were being robbed of their full inheritance, both now and in eternity, and wanted them to receive rewards for their well-spent and fruitful lives. Paul always had a long-term view, wanting what was best for his spiritual children in the light of eternity.

In an increasingly heartless and lonely world, the church should provide a contrast of intimate love and trust. We must learn to bear one another's burdens and weep with those who weep. As God enlarges churches to impact society, we must never lose the crucial place of the small group network. As John Stott says, 'I do not think it is an exaggeration to say that small groups, Christian family or fellowship groups, are indispensable for our growth into spiritual maturity.' (John R. W. Stott, *One People*, Falcon Books, 1969)

Discipleship was modelled for us by Jesus in a small group setting. He took twelve men and apprenticed them, promising that he would make them fishers of men. His purpose was not to entertain them but to train and transform them. Sadly, over the centuries our expectation of church life has been drastically changed. Now our church services have developed an 'audience' mentality where observation has replaced participation and platform performances can replace training.

I was once preaching at Covenant Life Church in the Washington DC area. It had been a good meeting and the large congregation applauded generously at the end of my sermon. Their leader, my great friend CJ Mahaney, then asked, 'How many have been blessed this morning?' Hundreds shouted enthusiastically that they had. He then amazed the congregation by telling them that they were totally deceived.

Everybody was taken aback. What had I said to deceive them? Thankfully he quickly explained that Jesus said, 'Now that you know these things, you will be blessed if you *do* them' (Jn 13:17).

He then pinpointed the great danger of thinking you have been blessed merely by hearing. Hearing is a stepping stone. It opens the way to doing and to the blessing that follows doing. Our danger is that instead of being trained and 'prepared for works of service' (Eph 4:12), we become mere consumers who evaluate church life by the wrong criteria. Discipleship is crucial if we are going to produce the real thing, and small cell groups are surely the best context for this process so that openness and accountability can develop and training can take place.

Without these principles in place we may still become a large congregation but people may gather for the wrong reason, be trained to do nothing and leave when the they feel like it. In real terms such attenders add nothing to the resources of the local church. They have not been partakers in any kind of discipling and are bearing no fruit that counts.

Henry G. Bosch tells the amusing story of what happened when a customer in a small store discovered that 'Eddie' the slow moving clerk was not around.

'Where's Eddie? Is he sick?'
'Nope,' came the reply. 'He ain't working here no more.'
'Do you have anyone in mind for the vacancy?' enquired the customer.
'Nope! Eddie didn't leave no vacancy!'
(H. G. Bosch *He Left No Vacancy*, Our Daily Bread, May 1974, quoted by William A Beckham in *The Second Reformation* Touch Publications 1995)

The church described in Ephesians 4 is a many-membered body where each part is working properly so that the absence of any living member should be felt and regretted. When every member is working properly we shall see a mature church as Jesus desired she should be.

A house of prayer

'My [Father's] house will be called a house of prayer' (Mt 21:13). A biblical church will have a strong prayer emphasis. The early church devoted itself to prayer. Jesus modelled a life full of prayer and his disciples tried to emulate him. Churches must do the same.

Evangelical churches in the UK have always had their regular prayer meeting. Many of the so-called 'new churches' have replaced that with important house-group meetings, but this must not mean the abandoning of prayer! Corporate prayer is fundamental to the success of the local church. Through fervent believing prayer we affect local government decisions, promote godliness and righteousness in schools and bring about effective evangelistic breakthrough in our neighbourhood.

Prayer is a great weapon. Our prayer meetings should be the most important gatherings of the week, especially if we take spiritual warfare seriously. The local church is a body of disciples, an army at its best when its members pray fervently together.

You may say, 'I rarely go to the prayer meeting. My weekly schedule is too full.' If that is so, you must make radical changes! Prayer is the life-blood of the biblical church. If you do not take part in the regular corporate prayer life of your church, I urge you to change your programme and make it a top priority. We shall return to this theme in a later chapter.

A centre for evangelism

'The Lord's message rang out from you ... your faith in God has become known everywhere' (1 Thess 1:8). A biblical church should be a lively and powerful centre of evangelistic activity. If it isn't, many of the young people will leave in order to join a zealous evangelistic group. But the local church is by far the best context for aggressive evangelism and the receiving of new converts.

A church which emphasises the vital place of relationships and delights in charismatic worship can easily forget the commission to preach the gospel. When you stop reaching the lost, you thwart God's call on your life and grow spiritually sick. Preoccupied with small internal difficulties, you fail to motivate the next generation. Churches that become actively involved in evangelism find their young people have come alive spiritually. Many of them are not yet deeply experienced in the things of God, but they know Jesus and want to share him with their generation. But evangelism isn't the responsibility only of the young. A vibrant local church can discover all kinds of creative ways to penetrate our modern society with the good news – mums and toddlers' groups, businessmen's dinners, or keep-fit clubs. A biblical church will put a high commitment on gospel proclamation and the winning and discipling of converts.

Many churches are finding that their housegroups, which were formerly exclusively inward looking, can become excellent centres to promote evangelistic zeal and activity. By turning them into fellowship groups for outreach and multiplication we transform their style. They become cells whose main preoccupation is winning the lost – family fishing units.

When we think of fishing we often imagine a lonely individual sitting with his rod and line, hoping for the occasional catch. Bringing this imagery to mind when considering Jesus' words, 'I will make you fishers of men', we can construct a totally wrong picture. Instead we should imagine 'family fishing', which was Peter's and Andrew's and also James' and John's previous employment, involving nets and partnership. While in India I have watched family fishing take place. In that context a large net is slowly pulled to the shore by the men. Then the whole family of women and children become involved as the fish are landed on the beach.

Peter and John had been partners (Greek *koinonos*). as fishermen (Lk 5:10). Now they were to develop their fellowship (Greek *kiononia*) as fishers of men. When Jesus called them they had been 'preparing (Greek *katartizo*) their nets' (Mk 1:19). From now on they were to 'prepare (same Greek word *katartizo)* God's people for works of service' (Eph 4:12).

Net preparation, or mending, was part of the family fishing business. Net mending was not an end in itself. It was not a full-time job. They were not net-menders. They were fishermen! Once mended, the nets were to be swiftly used again. So it is with the church. God's people are to be 'mended' or 'prepared' not simply for the sake of being mended, but to become active participators in the family fishing business.

Every army on active service will need a small hospital unit. Bodies that have been damaged must be mended again and loving care must be administered. The danger is when we turn the whole army into a hospital and change the atmosphere of the church. Sadly the church has often been seen exclusively as a place of healing rather than a place of preparation for works of service.

A centre for worship

A biblical church is also a worshipping church. Worship is our highest calling. We are a royal priesthood who offer spiritual sacrifices acceptable to God. He saved you for his own pleasure and wants to receive your love and to delight in your worship. Church-based evangelism is an endeavour to gather more worshippers for God. As John Piper says, 'Where passion for God is weak, zeal for missions will be weak. Churches that are not centred on the exaltation of the majesty and beauty of God will scarcely kindle a fervent desire to declare his glory among the nations ... You cannot commend what you don't cherish ... God is most glorified in us when we are most satisfied in him' (John Piper, *Let the Nations Be Glad*, IVP). A worship service where you do not experience heartfelt personal fellowship with Jesus is a sad meeting. Services like this are not worth attending. Your personal devotion to Jesus, expressed in times of glorious worship, are central to your whole Christian experience.

Heartfelt worship is the mainspring of all other Christian activity and aspiration. As J. I. Packer said, 'The life of true holiness is rooted in the soil of awed adoration. It does not grow elsewhere. That which grows elsewhere is not true holiness, whatever else it is. No blend of zeal, passion, self-denial, discipline, orthodoxy and effort adds up to holiness where praise is lacking' (J. I. Packer, *A Passion for Holiness*, Crossway Books, 1992). When we assemble, our goal is to meet with God himself, so we must make room for his glory to be revealed. Fresh encounters with the living God will transform your life. Keep clear of any restrictive liturgies and beware of leaning too heavily on the preparation of gifted musicians. They must help, not hinder us.

It's so easy to fall short of God's best. Simply singing the most up-to-date new worship songs in pleasant succession is not the ultimate aim. We want to bring our personal and corporate devotion to God, to linger in his presence and satisfy his heart with our love. To this end we are invited to declare his praise and to enter within the veil to express our adoration.

In such a setting we should expect God to manifest himself to us. We are in an intimate relationship with him. He is our Father; we are his children. Christ is our bridegroom; we are his bride. The Holy Spirit is present, wanting to make these realities come alive to us, so that we emerge having given God the glory due to his name and having received inner renewal and strength from him. Worship leaders interjecting little sermons and exhortations between songs do not help us to express our love to God. As groups of Spirit-filled believers, we must make room for the Holy Spirit's ministry in our hearts. As he prompts one here and another there, the body described in 1 Corinthians 12:12–14 will begin to function as he directs. Most of us are members of churches whose size is ideal for the regular occurrence of this biblical style of worship, where many can take part and there is no unnecessary dependence on being led from the front through a PA system. Beware the danger of losing spontaneity and the inspiration and interruptions of the Holy Spirit.

Churches that are too big to allow the full expression of this kind of worship in their Sunday meetings must do two things. First, their members need to enjoy corporate Spirit-led worship in smaller groupings within the church. Second, those who take responsibility for leading the worship in the larger celebration must get as near as possible to the underlying principles that apply to the smaller setting.

God is still seeking fellowship with his children in the large celebration. His people still crave intimacy with him and the Holy Spirit is still powerfully present. We must give him space to do the unpredictable. If we organise him out of our meetings, we will lose much that was regained in the battle for a New Testament style of worship. We will gradually cease to be genuinely charismatic in our worship, and our expectation of the immediacy of God's presence will gradually fade.

We are called to build biblical churches: groups of believers whose God is working powerfully in every activity mentioned here. The church is his vehicle for answering the world's needs; his strategy for reaching all the families of the earth. May he help us to build biblically and to glorify his name in our generation.

THE CHURCH –
THROUGH AN
APOSTLE'S EYES

J esus revolutionised the thinking of his contemporaries when
he taught them to call God 'Father'. To them, God had been
distant and fearful, not intimate and knowable. Jesus assured
his followers that their heavenly Father knew their needs and
delighted in meeting them. He introduced a 'family atmosphere'
to prayer. The new community he formed enjoyed intimacy with
God and with one another.

Following Jesus' example, Paul and the other early apostles
laid a foundation of love and friendship in the churches by their
style. They were not remote rabbis or distant priests. Paul came
among the churches as a father, and when he left them they wept.
When he wrote to them he addressed them in the tenderest terms.

The world around us longs for intimacy. People look for
love and are bewildered by their experiences. They feel let down,
used, robbed and spoiled. In this computer age they lack personal
significance and value. Is there no one at home in the universe?
The gospel not only tells us that there is a God in heaven, but
also that there is a family on earth to which we can belong, and
leaders who know how to build not remote faceless congregations
but loving caring communities.

When I was first converted I found it extremely difficult
to penetrate church life as it was then expressed. It seemed so
formal and distant. Obviously comparative strangers, people
greeted one another at the door with correct handshakes. Actually

they only seemed to shake one person's hand and that was the pastor's as they left the building. Formal clothing, solid pews, old-fashioned music, hushed atmosphere, unreal antiquated language – all conspired to alienate me rather than welcome me to this new and frightening territory. Gradually I learned how to conduct myself and was taught the 'language of Zion'. Little by little the metamorphosis was taking place. I guessed that this was what it meant to be a Christian. It was all new to me, so I had to knuckle under and learn.

At the same time other longings were striving in my heart. Surely the good friendships I had enjoyed with my ungodly friends in the world should be surpassed in the church. If this is God's family, shouldn't it be better, richer and more meaningful, instead of unreal, religious and distant? It was so different in the Bible.

If we are going to reach our generation with the gospel and build churches that are relevant to our contemporaries and true to Scripture, we must rediscover the style of New Testament Christianity.

Genuine brothers

When Paul wrote to his friends at Philippi, he communicated so much of God's attitude and was transparent about his own feelings for them. He wrote to them as his brothers, his beloved, his longed for, his joy and his crown (Phil 4:1). Though Paul was a mighty apostle and arguably the greatest Christian leader of all time, he addressed the Christians at Philippi first as his 'brothers'. No clergy/laity divide in Paul's mind. Although he argued in 1 Corinthians 12 that 'God has set in the church first apostles', he did not stand aloof. In the church of Jesus Christ all are brothers! Jesus himself introduced the wonder of this new relationship when he said, 'Go instead to my brothers and tell them, "I am returning to my Father and your Father, to my God and your God"' (Jn 20:17). He isn't ashamed to call us brothers (Hebrews); he is the firstborn among many brothers. Brothers can relax together and joke together, and they do not even have to call one another 'brother Terry' or 'brother John'. I have four sons and I have never heard one of them call another 'brother Tim' or 'brother Simon'.

As Rob Warner has said, 'There are still churches where first names are never mentioned in the notices. Collecting the offering has the formal precision of a military exercise, and communion is distributed with the co-ordinated stiffness and unreality of a synchronised swimming team' (Rob Warner, *21st Century Church*, Hodder & Stoughton, 1993).

My former pastor was shocked that I refused to wear a clerical collar and amazed that I invited the church members to call me by my Christian name. He feared I would earn no respect from my congregation if I did not retain the normal trappings of the ministry. At Bible college I was told I should not form friendships with anyone in the congregation. If I wanted a friend I should seek out a pastor in a neighbouring town! 'Distance yourself!' But God wants a family that is built on loving relationships.

Heartfelt love

Paul called the Philippians 'my beloved'. No embarrassment clouded the issue. He loved them and wanted them to know it. It is wonderful to be loved and to have the liberty to express love to others. Do you ever tell other believers that you love them? I do not mean in that unreal way in which charismatics are sometimes called upon by the meeting leader to turn to the person sitting next to them and repeat parrot-like some terms of endearment. I am told that the sadly missed David Watson was once in a meeting where all present were exhorted to turn to their immediate neighbour with the words, 'I can't live without you.' He turned and discovered to his dismay that he was standing next to a very beautiful blonde young woman. He could not bring himself to express the required declaration of personal devotion!

There are, nevertheless, many opportunities when believers can plainly tell others of their love. Paul frequently did so and called God to be his witness on one occasion (see 2 Corinthians 11:11). Relationships of love modelled by leaders are of enormous value in setting the style for church life. Many in the modern world feel terribly unloved. It is wonderful when we can honestly express our heartfelt love to one another — not as sentimental superficial jargon, but out of developing relationships of trust, appreciation, respect and delight.

Longed for

Paul longed for his friends at Philippi. He called them 'my longed for'. He had zealous ambition for them; he longed to see them, be with them, inspire their progress, help them stand. He longed for them not simply from his own human resources of affection, but with the passion of Christ. In the opening remarks of his letter he spoke of experiencing longings for them with all the inner yearnings of Christ (Phil 1). Christ's love and zeal for them were burning in Paul's heart.

This kind of language is far removed from much modern church life, where correctness and balance prevail and cordial affection has replaced passion. If we keep opening our hearts to the Holy Spirit he will pour God's love into them, rekindling the kind of love that he so desires in his church. Wholehearted love is his desired norm. He wants nothing less in our ranks. Lukewarmness is anathema to him. He is sickened by it.

My joy

Next, Paul saw them as his 'joy'. He delighted in them. He did not constantly complain about the shortcomings of the churches he served. Rather he commended them and flooded them with affection and grace. We might argue that it was one thing to rejoice over the Philippian church, but what about others like Corinth? Was he equally affirming about all the churches? To our surprise we discover that before he corrected the wayward Corinthians he first affirmed them and rejoiced in their lacking no gift. He did not correct them in order to shame them, but rather to exhort them as his dear children. They had many tutors but not many fathers. If to others he was not an apostle, he was to them. He calls them 'the proof' of his apostolic ministry.

Imagine citing the Corinthian church as proof of your apostleship! Here was a church involved in incest, drunkenness at the Lord's table, divisiveness, carnality, wrong handling of charismatic gifts, pride and more, but Paul called them the proof of his apostolic ministry! He owned them and loved them, even though he longed for them to change. He did not disown them; they were his children in the Lord. They also, like Philippi, were his joy.

It is so easy for Christian leaders to create the wrong ethos in the church. Constant exhortations and heavy-handed manipulation become the norm in some congregations. Many languish under a cloud of condemnation intensified by preaching, which only adds burdens. Many a believer is crushed by a vague sense of inadequacy, of not producing enough or not being worthy of God's affirmation. How believers need to hear the kind of unequivocal statements that Paul loved to shout from the house tops; namely that nothing can separate us from the love of Christ! If God is for us who is against us (Rom 8)? Many believers desperately need to know for certain what the psalmist knew when he joyfully sang, 'This I know – God is for me!'

The church is God's joy. She is the joy of all the earth (Ps 48:2). First God tells us what we are by his grace – his joy! Then he helps us to live accordingly. Grace lifts us, stirs hope in our hearts and inspires us to rise to our calling.

My crown

Finally Paul described the Philippians as his 'crown'. Not a royal crown, but a wreath of victory, something gained at the winning post. Paul always saw life in the context of 'prize day' before Christ at his coming. He constantly referred to that day when Christ would appear. His desire was to present a pure virgin to Christ; to present every man mature in him. They were his crown of rejoicing in that day!

With this in mind Paul urged those in his care to press on with all diligence. He did not see them as his short-term responsibility. He was not coldly professional – he saw himself as joined to people for the whole duration. Even when absent he held them in his heart. Paul looked forward to the crown. When writing to Timothy he had almost finished his course. He was not overwhelmed with nostalgia for the 'good old days', he was still looking forward. Having said he had finished the course his next few words were not 'in the past', but 'in the future'!

When Paul called the church at Philippi 'his crown' he was thinking of the future. In Philippians 2:16 he told them to hold fast to the word of life so that in the day of Christ he might have cause to glory because he did not run in vain or toil in vain. To the Thessalonians he said, 'For who is our hope or joy or crown of exultation? Is it not even you, in the presence of our Lord Jesus at His coming?' (1 Thess 2:19, NASB)

Paul was no time server or hireling. He was profoundly joined to those he cared for. They had lasting significance for him and he could not afford to play at religion. The progress of those in his charge mattered deeply. He was looking for the crown and in a mysterious way his crown was related to their progress and their ultimate success.

Many modern Christians have heard little about rewards, and rarely think of the great day of their presentation before Christ. Not so Paul. He kept that day in constant focus. He believed in rewards. His life service came before Ignatius of Loyola's famous prayer, 'Not looking for any reward save that of knowing I do thy will.' This may be a fine sounding sentiment, but it simply isn't a biblical one. Jesus said, 'I am coming soon! My reward is with me, and I will give to everyone according to what he has done' (Rev 22:12). It is not for you to be slightly embarrassed about the whole concept of rewards. It is hardly your place to correct Jesus and tell him that rewards are rather a shallow ethic and that you have risen above such things. Jesus wants to share the spoils of his victory and is committed to rewarding your works.

Paul knew that everything in this life was by grace, but God's grace was not in vain in his case since it motivated him to labour 'harder than all of them' (1 Cor 15:10). Paul's own example of passion and zeal helped to set the tone for the churches of his day. As a good leader he was always pressing on, longing to lay hold of that for which God had laid hold of him, not regarding himself as having arrived but pressing forward (Phil 3).

Leaders should provide an atmosphere of love and security, of affirmation and acceptance, of brotherly love and mutual delight, but they should also bring a sense of passionate commitment to Christ's cause. Christ wants a glorious and magnificent bride. Paul was determined to play his part in preparing one. He wanted the churches he served to be similarly passionate about the coming wedding day.

The presentation day consumed Paul's vision. He communicated that zeal not only in the grand sweep of his massive vision of the universal church, but by helping a group of believers at Philippi to understand that they also were part of it all. They were his brothers, his beloved, his longed-for, his joy and crown.

Although Paul was the outstanding apostle of the New Testament, his attitudes are not to be regarded as unique. This former cold-hearted Pharisee had been transformed by an encounter with Christ. Filled with the Holy Spirit, he became a channel of God's love to the churches. You can experience the same transformation. The Holy Spirit can flood your heart with love for other believers. Your church can be a centre of love, joy and delight. Forgiven much, you can learn to give away mercy freely. As the Holy Spirit is poured out in your church, you see how much God loves his people and treasures them in spite of their obvious weaknesses and failures. Become a giver of love in your church. Help it to become a place of love and peace – the loving family that people are longing to find.

BELONGING TO A
LOCAL CHURCH

Take her by the shoulders, look her in the eye and say, 'I promise I will never leave you for another woman.' Reassure her of your love. Express your commitment. What healing this should bring within a vulnerable marriage. How many children would love to hear their father solemnly guarantee that he would at no time desert them and their mother? When we honestly express our commitment we release such peace and joy in those we love. Anxiety is relieved and ground is secured on which we can build with assurance for the future.

Nobody wants to endure life crippled by uncertainty regarding the loyalty of the one they hold dear. When we give our love and devotion, our greatest longing is that it will be received tenderly, handled with care and thoroughly reciprocated. Surely the very foundation of our Christian security is the knowledge that God is totally committed to us. He has said, 'I will never fail you or forsake you.' We can rest assured that he is faithful. Because he is our sure and constant Shepherd, we can lie down in green pastures. He restores our soul.

Paul testified that he could face death daily and be more than a conqueror because he was convinced that nothing in all creation would be able to separate him from the love of God (Rom 8:38–39). With this assurance, Paul could confidently risk all kinds of dangers as he fulfilled his apostolic ministry. God's clear commitment to you releases you to enjoy your Christian life without tension, and motivates you to attempt great exploits for him, confident that he will not let you down.

Your reliability in relationships will inspire confidence and security in your colleagues. The whole church prospers when its members prove genuinely trustworthy. When Christians express their devotion to Christ by a dependable lifestyle, they bring a warm glow to the body of believers to whom they are joined. Lack of commitment is a blight on the body of Christ.

Some Christians don't feel the need to commit themselves to any local body of believers. They see themselves simply as members of the body of Christ at large and do not give their allegiance to any local assembly, thereby totally failing to grasp the fundamental purpose of body life as expressed in the New Testament. Jack Hayford in his book *The Church on the Way* tells how a guest at his church signed the visitors' book and beside her name indicated her home church to be 'the body of Christ'. For its address, she added 'worldwide'. I guess her name appeared on no one's washing-up rota!

R. C. Sproul uncompromisingly states,

> It is both foolish and wicked to suppose that we will make much progress in sanctification if we isolate ourselves from the visible church. Indeed it is commonplace to hear people declare that they don't need to unite with a church to be a Christian. They claim that their devotion is personal and private, not institutional or corporate. This is not the testimony of the great saints of history; it is the confession of fools. (R. C. Sproul, *The Soul's Quest for God*, Tyndale House, 1992)

They devoted themselves

A phrase frequently used in the New Testament to describe people's response to the gospel is that they 'were added' to the church. They did not simply get right with God; they were added to the company of disciples who devoted themselves to the apostles' doctrine, fellowship, breaking of bread and prayer (Acts 2:42).

The early Christians were devoted to fellowship. They were constantly together and relinquished the right to individualism and selfishness by no longer regarding the things they possessed as their own. There was no coercion. People had glad and generous hearts. They expressed commitment to one another as a spontaneous outworking of their new life in Christ. Their dynamic encounter with God drew them together in an intimacy of fellowship which made their previous experience of synagogue attendance pale into insignificance. They had all been drinking of the same Spirit and were all captivated by the same Jesus. They wanted to work out their new life by a thoroughgoing expression of love and loyalty to one another.

Many of us who grew up in the impersonal church-going often experienced within English Christianity, have been thrilled by the new breakthrough of loving personal involvement associated with the so-called 'house-church movement'. Although that title is now an outdated misnomer (being replaced by 'new churches'), the truth is that in the early days, an almost indefinable development took place as many transferred their experience of church from the pew to their own front room. A new intimacy replaced the old formality and a foundation was laid that has not been lost as we have outgrown our lounges and moved into larger meeting places. Relaxed friendliness has replaced the unreality that was so often associated with the religious atmosphere of the 'sanctuary'. Personal loyalty has superseded mere outward conformity.

There is something very attractive about close friends who trust each other, enjoy one another's presence and really care sacrificially for one another's well being. Loneliness holds little to attract us. We might occasionally crave some solitude, but eight discs, a favourite book and a luxury item would hardly suffice to lure most of us to a desert island for the rest of our lives. We like company. Real friendship is a beautiful thing, but like most beautiful things it does not come cheaply. It is possible to be a Christian and yet be devoid of satisfying friendships.

Adrian Plass has hilariously found us out for all our sham and unreality and we would do well to learn from his inspired mocking. A more relaxed church life does not inevitably lead to deeper friendships. Many still battle with shyness, superficiality and the kind of human contact that leaves us lonely in the crowd.

So how do we make and keep friends? The King James translation of Proverbs 18:24 reads, 'A man that has friends must show himself friendly.' Although this rendering has been abandoned by more recent versions of the Bible, it nevertheless makes an obvious and helpful point. Some people lack friends because of their own unfriendly ways.

When we send out unfriendly vibes we will attract few close companions. If we are critical and hostile, few will seek our company. If you try to build relationships with others by giving them a display of your cutting humour towards a third party, don't be surprised if few entrust their secrets to you.

Friendship flourishes with those who accept others warmly and affirm them. We want to escape our loneliness by finding people with whom we can share our most intimate hopes and fears. It is only as we 'open up' our hearts that we find the true release that friendship can provide.

Have hours of Christian counselling come to replace the joys of good honest friendship? If we do not rediscover the comforts of deep and open Christian friendship I fear that counselling specialists will multiply and intimacy will be by appointment! People who are gifted in counselling and willing to give their hours sacrificially to help the needy members of our churches will be in danger of supplying an escape from loneliness, instead of providing the specialist insights that they are peculiarly gifted to offer to the most needy.

If mutual acceptance opens the door to friendship, loyalty under pressure provides the means for keeping it open. If I share my secrets with you I want to know I can trust you. I also want to know that you will be faithful to me even if I let you down. This requires enormous discipline in a world of disloyalty and in a context where Satan, the most disloyal creature in the universe, is committed to destroying everything beautiful. He hates covenant love and is aiming to make it scarce on planet earth!

How often friendships are lost because we fail to remember Satan's active hostility! How he loves to sow the seeds of doubt and distrust! He knows his only hope is to divide and conquer. If we remain loyal and true to one another his hands are tied.

Loyalty means that I will stick with you even when I know your faults. Uncovering your hidden weakness will not make me forsake our friendship but will simply provide more motivation to pray and talk openly. True friendship has no time for 'no go areas'. We must be free to talk about anything, yet not force the pace too quickly. Some have been deeply hurt by previous experiences and find it difficult to open up again. Nothing should be taken for granted as we progress towards full openness and transparency in our friendships. We need time together where there is opportunity to unwind and develop beyond the superficial.

If laughter is medicine to bring you healing, laughter with others is a feast for your soul to build you up. True friends will weep with those who weep and laugh with those who laugh. We need time for both, and the mutual knowledge that makes it possible. It is too easy to hide behind our religious façade and miss life's best.

In reality, Christians have a capacity for friendship which goes way beyond others' because we have a high and yet compassionate view of mankind. We know that people are worth it! Many of our contemporaries doubt that. Some see men as merely advanced animals, simply responding to various stimuli. Jean-Paul Sartre regarded humanity as 'trash'. Others experience sudden painful failure in their companions and are shocked and disillusioned by the sin factor, so that they give up on people.

Christians are uniquely clear about the nature of man. We know before we start on a friendship that this person will probably occasionally let us down. We understand this. We know that even Christians have their treasure in clay pots and although we often contact the treasure we sometimes come up against the clay pot! Christians should be somewhat unshockable and therefore able to sustain friendship. We know about the apostle Peter's denial and King David's adultery. We understand flesh and blood.

We also understand grace and redemption and realise that we are being changed from glory to glory. Loyalty can be maintained even through painful failure. With God's help, bitterness and resentment can be overcome and discarded. We can always find grace to start again in a way that the unredeemed know nothing about.

Christians are also in a unique place to display friendship between the sexes. Free from male chauvinism they can love, honour and respect friends of the opposite sex with great joy and fulfilment. Modern society, with its preoccupation with either sexual immorality or sexist rivalry, has made it very difficult for men and women to develop good healthy friendships between the sexes that are free from undercurrents. Christians should be able to relax into excellent friendships with the opposite sex. Jesus loved not only Lazarus but also Mary and Martha. We can be free to love our brothers and sisters with equal joy and purity.

It is so easy to use people and drop people, to be offended by people and then prove disloyal at their time of need. Proverbs says, 'A friend loves at all times.' Let's make sure that we make and keep friends well.

We have begun to understand that God's church is a family and that family relationships are appropriate in the house of God. We are not simply a number of lonely Christian pilgrims who happen to gather at the same place of worship every Sunday. Like the early church, we feel our lives are interwoven in a personal fellowship and love founded on relationships, not church programmes and buildings.

We have also seen the importance of inviting prospective new members to consider these values before throwing in their lot with us. Early on, while the whole church could still meet in our front room, this was hardly necessary, but now we have grown numerically and others have found our church lifestyle attractive. To retain the same church ethos and philosophy, it is crucial that the foundations of our fellowship are clearly understood – hence we ask prospective members to weigh up our value system before joining. We want them to hold dear the distinctives that excite and motivate us. We want them to be added like the 3,000 were added in the book of Acts. The values that the 120 held through their association with Jesus were thoroughly imparted to the 3,000 who joined the church overnight.

Radical commitment

The singleness of purpose of the 120 was captured by the 3,000. They all devoted themselves to the apostles' doctrine, fellowship, breaking of bread and prayers. There seemed to be no casual discipleship. Everybody was devoted. The unique chemistry of unity enjoyed by the 120 was fully embraced by the 3,000, so that they were all of one heart and one mind. This wholehearted devotion had its roots in a radical commitment to Christ. It is impossible to build church commitment into people who have not first given themselves to Christ.

Paul reported glowingly about the Macedonian churches that 'they gave themselves first to the Lord and then to us in keeping with God's will' (2 Cor 8:5). Both ingredients are essential. You must give yourself unreservedly to Christ. If you fail to take that step and simply want to be a casual church-goer, you will find a company of committed disciples difficult to handle. But if you have abandoned yourself to Jesus Christ as Lord, you will automatically want to find a way to work out your devotion to him, and the appropriate setting for that outworking is the local body of believers.

The early church was knit together with intimate bonds of fellowship. Many Christians today are rejoicing to rediscover a church life based on the New Testament model. Each local church should function like a body – 'joined and held together by every supporting ligament, grow[ing] and build[ing] itself up in love, as each part does its work' (Eph 4:16). Initial commitment must then be followed by ongoing commitment to walking in the light with your new-found brothers and sisters. You must devote yourselves to fellowship. As John Stott says, 'If the church is central to God's purpose, as seen in both history and the gospel, it must surely also be central to our lives. How can we take lightly what God takes so seriously? How dare we push to the circumference what God has placed at the centre?' (John R. W. Stott, *The Message of Ephesians*, from The Bible Speaks Today series, IVP, 1979).

Modern Western society is characterised by selfishness and isolation. It will require application on your part to devote yourself to fellowship. Often the television and the armchair will be the soft option, luring you away from opportunities of fellowship at house group or elsewhere. Frequently the temptation to be disloyal will creep up on you and gossip will attract you like juicy morsels. All your saliva glands will start pumping as the familiar words reach your ears: 'Have you heard ...?' It will require devotion to fellowship and commitment to God's purposes to refuse to hear rumours or take part in backbiting and criticism.

As Paul Billheimer said, 'In spite of all her lamentable weaknesses, appalling failures and indefensible shortcomings, the Church is the mightiest force for civilisation' (Paul Billheimer, *Destined for the Throne*, CLC).

Are you devoted to fellowship? Are you committed to walking in excellent relationships with your local body of believers? If not, how are you working out your devotion to Christ? Have you found another way? Freelance Christianity is much easier, but it won't build the church and it won't turn the nation to God.

THE CHURCH AT PRAYER

What a sight it must have been! Tables upturned, coins scattered, livestock fleeing and Jesus standing with whip in hand at the centre of all the commotion. Dismissing the religious façade of special temple money and sacrifices, he declared it 'a robbers' den'. Then, full of zeal for his Father's house, he reminded them of God's word on the matter: 'My house will be called a house of prayer' (Mt 21:13).

He surely could have described the house of God in many other ways, so we should take serious note of this particular title. Prayer is seen as the distinctive feature of the house of God. Now we are his house (Heb 3:6) and the question must be faced: To what degree could our life together be called a house of prayer?

A few years ago one would often assess the spiritual zeal of a local church by looking at its notice-board to see if and when it held prayer meetings. I was raised in a church which had two evening prayer meetings in its weekly programme and I followed that pattern in my first pastorate. Sadly, these prayer meetings were often formal and lifeless. As time went by God began to speak to us about the essential place of cell groups in our body life, and the home-group system replaced the church prayer meeting and Bible study evening. Though these home meetings were to include prayer, we made it perfectly clear that they were not prayer meetings. Their purpose was more diverse, covering many aspects of our corporate life. Prayers offered in them have often centred more around the personal needs and aspirations of the cell members. This has proved a great and necessary blessing in building the lives of the members together far more intimately. Formality has disappeared as lives have become open to one another.

As time has passed, however, the criticism could be levelled that we are no longer essentially a house of prayer. A house of fellowship, yes, or even a house of praise, but not a house of prayer. Now God has impressed on us the need to rediscover corporate prayer – not in place of our cell life, but in addition to it.

Spiritual warfare

There is a growing consciousness of spiritual warfare in the modern church, and the word 'revival' has been on our lips again. If we are going to see a powerful spiritual breakthrough, we will have to develop in intercession.

'Why prayer is so indispensable we cannot say, but we had better recognise the fact even if we cannot explain it,' wrote J. O. Fraser, the mighty pioneer missionary who so proved God among the Lisu tribes of China some sixty years ago, resulting in the conversion of thousands.

Fraser had a highly developed understanding of the power of prayer. He approached the whole matter very pragmatically when he said: 'We often speak of intercessory work as being of vital importance. I want to prove that I believe this in actual fact by giving my first and best energies to it as God may lead. I feel like a businessman who perceives that a certain line of goods pays better than any other in his store and who purposes making it his chief investment' (Eileen Crossman, *Mountain Rain*, OMF Books, 1982).

Having temporarily abandoned the church prayer meeting, its rediscovery had to be in keeping with all that God had taught us in the intervening years.

We begin with praise, seeing the Lord high and lifted up above all our needs and longings, able to supply every answer. But we remember on such occasions that we have come primarily to intercede. Without this discipline we can too easily get carried away with praise (a glorious preoccupation!) and find no time to ask, seek and knock. By all means we let our evening be punctuated by moments of believing praise. Then we return to the job in hand with disciplined purpose. When we have the assurance that we have been heard, we conclude the time with a confident shout of thanksgiving!

It goes without saying that we must be a people of true unity of heart to release power in prayer, not seeking to impress with our eloquence, nor imposing guilt with our burden, nor despising the faltering words of those new to the experience. Eloquence can often replace childlike and genuine faith, while the newest convert can often bring a note of raw reality which helps us all break through. The prayer meeting, therefore, must be a place where genuine love is expressed.

Sometimes we do not have enough time to wait for everyone to add their prayers to a consecutive chain and so we feel free to raise our voices all together in pursuit of our theme. God can untangle our cries. Then someone may find the anointing to lead in prayer in summary of our corporate burden.

Elders must be open before God to get a sense of direction for corporate prayer and must be unafraid to lead, letting others catch their burden. It is often through the lack of clear goals that prayer is dissipated. Where relationships are well formed and love prevails, they are able to bring teaching and admonition to those who pray 'off centre' prayers, or who want to include every burden in one long list of a prayer. Without instruction we fail to see issues through.

We are in a battle and often we need to hold ground until faith assures us we have what we ask for. The fact that someone has just prayed your prayer is no reason for you not to pray it as well. Joash learned from Elisha that sometimes, to prevail in the warfare, you must strike five or six times and not give up after three attempts (2 Kings 13:19). Learning to use the weapons of our warfare which are able to pull down enemy strongholds, we become increasingly aware of our army status, moving together in throwing back the powers of darkness and bringing in the rule of Christ through militant faith.

A number of books have been written on spiritual warfare in the last decade. Often this has led to very speculative ideas of how prayer should be conducted. As George Mallone has said,

> A mistaken and unbiblical trend towards dualism is developing in today's literature on spiritual warfare. Instead of producing faith in God's overcoming ability, some works instil fear. The Bible views Satan as a weak shadowy figure, who stays in the background whenever God is doing his glorious work – not as one who has an equal amount of power. Satan is no match for God. We are to give him no glory by fearing his works or power. (George Mallone, *Arming for Spiritual Warfare*, IVP, 1991)

Some believers seem to see every delay or difficulty as part of Satan's work and this subsequently leads to Satan being directly addressed so that his power in a situation can be broken. This is out of step with the prayers of the early apostles recorded, for instance, in Acts 4. Some teachers seem to suggest that the early apostles, thwarted by opposition to their preaching in Jerusalem, should have 'bound the spirit over Jerusalem' in order to proceed with their kingdom work. No such prayer is recorded. These early believers were very conscious of who was in charge of the situation. They called out with one voice to the 'sovereign Lord' and saw his power released. They did not become preoccupied with addressing a mystical force which was supposedly over Jerusalem frustrating their advance.

Surely prayers should always be offered to God. The apostles' appeal for boldness was answered in a dramatic way and the power of God was unleashed again so that they continued boldly to preach Christ. When Paul and Silas found that their initial invasion of Europe was withstood, resulting in their being put into prison in Philippi, we again see no preoccupation with Satan, but men in an inner prison singing their praises to God, which again led to a massive display of God's power and a further advance of the gospel. Undoubtedly there is much to learn about spiritual warfare but it is important we catch the atmosphere of the New Testament and learn from the apostles rather than invent a new style of praying which seems to be foreign to Scripture and also brings a lot of focus to Satan himself.

Open to the Holy Spirit

Throughout the recent outpourings of the Holy Spirit we have found our prayer meetings taking on a new dimension. For example, intercession for a planned project can often give way to sudden outbreaks of Holy Spirit activity. These sometimes take the form of particular prayer for the individuals responsible for an upcoming event. Instead of simply praying for the intended programme, we often find ourselves praying for those who will be taking responsibility on the day. This often results in a fresh outpouring of power on these people. A kind of spiritual release can then take place where many begin to have fresh encounters with the Holy Spirit.

At this point we very much make it our aim to be sensitive to what the Holy Spirit has come to do among us at this particular time. Individuals are often prompted to pray for others, bringing them scriptures, particular exhortations or prophecies. This can result in the prayer meeting 'breaking up' for a while as the power of God is manifested upon people, but this does not necessarily mean that corporate intercession is now over. We may well return to united praying again later, or groups around the room can be interceding together while others are laying hands on one another.

In this context, the gifts of the Holy Spirit are not playthings but powerful weapons in the battle. Visions and prophecies often lead us in the conflict and give us a sense of direction.

Prayer and action

It is a tragedy that anyone should regard prayer meetings as boring. Sadly, this often used to be the case, with a deadly sense of going through a routine that seemed unrelated to life. When we look at the prayer meetings in the book of Acts we always find them against a backcloth of action.

The Day of Pentecost started as a prayer meeting, but it was so related to action that it is impossible to discern when they ceased sitting in the house in prayer and came into the streets in power. The next recorded prayer meeting is preceded by a brief visit to jail and concludes with a shaking building crowded with people freshly refilled with the Holy Spirit.

After that, we find the church gathered at Mary's home because Peter is in prison again. It was concluded not by formal benediction, but by a released Peter, who actually found it more difficult to get into the prayer meeting than out of prison!

Another prayer meeting in Antioch witnessed the call and commissioning of Paul and Barnabas to their apostolic work. Constantly prayer meetings were alive with the interventions of God.

Our times of church prayer should be part of our corporate lifestyle based on prophetic vision. If our local church is inactive and merely ticking over, the prayer meeting will reflect that in a lack of purpose and life. But if we are a people moving forward in God's purpose, our praying will be relevant and exciting. Evangelistic endeavour, special outreach, a need for miraculous provision of money, or some other goal will motivate us. Jesus said, 'Ask that you may receive that your joy may be full.'

The boredom associated with prayer meetings in the past has often been caused by their predictability and lack of living purpose. There was a Thursday night prayer meeting every week whether or not anything special was happening. Eventually, people just went through the motions.

Out of the rut

New Testament prayer meetings seem more spontaneous and related to life. Today in the West, our church notices rarely include reference to the pastor's recent imprisonment for preaching in the open air! But even if circumstances do not demand emergency prayer meetings, we can still change things around from time to time.

We have experimented with weeks of non-stop church prayer, with people signing up for selected hours through a seven-day chain of day and night intercession. The numbers present for each hour varied from one or two to a dozen or more, but there was a great sense of church unity as one took over the baton from another. A diary has been kept on any significant leading given by the Holy Spirit and what subjects have been particularly prayed through during each hour.

We have also divided a month between church house groups for days of prayer and fasting. Excluding the weekends, we appointed groups to a day each to maintain the chain. After a day of fasting, the groups gathered on their appropriate evening to pray. As the month passed the whole church was drawn into the prayer battle. Using many different approaches, more and more churches are feeling the call to rediscover corporate prayer.

As Colin Dye, the leader of the dynamic Kensington Temple, testifies,

> There is one Master Key and the Master Key belongs to the Master himself who shares it with us. Behind every successful development, every creative plan and every thrust forward there is and has always been one thing – earnest, sustained prayer. Prayer is the Master Key. It is of vital importance. I prize it above everything I do. If the Lord were to remove every other aspect of my ministry in

public, leaving only my call to intercede, I would be fully satisfied. Prayer is the creative powerhouse of God within us. Prayer effects real change. Prayer transforms lives, churches and communities. (Colin Dye, *Prayer Explosion*, Hodder & Stoughton, 1996)

We need revival

There are practical lessons to be learned, but let us be sure of this: revival is always preceded by strong corporate prayer and, indeed, has often broken out in the very prayer meetings themselves. We must keep adjusting our programmes in response to the leading of the Holy Spirit and have growing expectation for a genuine visitation of God. I thank God for the refreshing we are enjoying today, but it is by no means the revival we so desperately need.

If we are to see full revival blessing we must rediscover the kind of prayer commitment expressed by previous generations. It is so inspiring to read about revivals of the past, rubbing shoulders, for instance, with such men as Jeremiah Lamphier, the city missionary who started a weekly lunchtime prayer meeting in New York and saw it grow from six people on its first meeting to twenty in its second: '... the famous Fulton Street prayer meeting had begun. The first week in October it was decided to hold the meeting daily instead of weekly, and within six months ten thousand businessmen were meeting every day to pray for revival. Within two years a million converts had been added to the American churches' (Brian H. Edwards, *Revival*, Evangelical Press, 1990).

As Thomas Charles, another great hero of past revival, said, 'Unless we are favoured with frequent revivals, and a strong, powerful work of the Holy Spirit of God, we shall in great degree degenerate, and have only a name to live; religion will soon lose its vigour; the ministry will hardly retain its lustre and glory; and iniquity will, of consequence, abound' (*Ibid*).

Or as Arthur Wallis, a great hero and former friend of mine, used to say, 'A movement of God will last as long as the spirit of prayer that inspired it.' May God continue to stir and inspire us to increasingly fervent prayer to see the outpouring of the Spirit on a believing, worshipful church and, as a result, see nations turning again to God.

THE CHURCH
A CENTRE FOR WORSHIP

One day Jesus looked for a worshipper – not in the temple or synagogue – but at a well, where a woman of doubtful morality was drawing water. The teaching he gave her has become fundamental to our understanding of true worship. The woman's preoccupation was with the correct location for worship – Jerusalem or Samaria. Jesus swept this away, revealing God's true priorities. God is Spirit and we must worship him, not in special places, but in Spirit and truth.

What did Jesus mean by worship in Spirit? The answer could be found in something else he said, 'These people honour me with their lips, but their hearts are far from me' (Mt 15:8). Worship without heart involvement is unacceptable to God. John Piper says, 'Where feelings for God are dead, worship is dead' (John Piper, *Desiring God*, IVP, 1989).

Thanks a lot

Jesus wants us to express our appreciation. Thanksgiving is an appropriate attitude towards God. J. I. Packer says, 'No religion anywhere has ever laid such stress on the need for thanksgiving, nor called on its adherents so incessantly and insistently to give God thanks as does the religion of the Bible' (J. I. Packer, *A Passion for Holiness*, Crossway Books, 1992).

Paul taught that man's rebellion against God began with failure to express thanks. 'Although they knew God, they neither glorified him as God nor gave thanks to him' (Rom 1:21). Lack of gratitude characterises the unbeliever who fails to acknowledge God and his standards of righteousness, as Paul goes on to say in Romans 1. Christians should stand in stark contrast, constantly expressing their thankfulness to God for who he is and what he's done. As we do this, our thanksgiving will be replaced by praise.

'Well played!' 'Great shot!' 'Wonderful meal!' 'You look magnificent!' We praise others for many reasons and enjoy expressing approval – it's part of our emotional fulfilment. God wants us to praise him continually. John Piper, in his outstanding book *Desiring God*, says that we tend to dislike people who crave praise or plaudits, wondering what's wrong with them. He says, 'We admire people who are secure and composed enough that they don't need to shore up their weaknesses and compensate for their deficiencies by trying to get compliments.'

So why does God want our praise? Piper continues:

> God is not weak and has no deficiencies. 'All things are from him and through him and to him' (Rom 11:36). 'He is not served by human hands as though he needed anything since he himself gives to all men life and breath and everything' (Acts 17:25). Everything that exists owes its existence to him and no-one can add anything to him which is not already flowing from him. Therefore God's zeal to seek his own glory and to be praised by men cannot be owing to his need to shore up some weakness or compensate for some deficiency.

Piper argues that because God is unique and glorious it is appropriate for him to draw our attention and seek our praise. For,

> If God should turn away from himself as the source of infinite joy he would cease to be God. He would deny the

infinite worth of his own glory ... What could God give us
to enjoy that would prove him most loving? There is only
one possible answer, himself! If he withholds himself from
our contemplation and our companionship, no matter what
else he gives us he is not loving.

What's it all about?

Our praise is most heartfelt when our minds are engaged. While
I was in the USA I endured American football on television. My
untrained eye saw little to get excited about. Men crunched one
another with bone-shaking tackles and kept stopping the action.
Oh for some flowing soccer! My American friends might wait
eagerly for the Superbowl, but my praise was muted – most of
the time I didn't know what was happening.

Many praise God in a limited way because they have
never spent time getting to know him or what he has done.
Their thinking has been man-centred rather than God-centred.
'How can I be fulfilled, get my hurts healed, have a successful
marriage?' Even our worship can be self-centred: 'I like quiet,
gentle songs.' 'I prefer up-tempo celebration praise.'

Worshippers must be preoccupied with the object of
their worship. Some people foolishly say, 'I don't want to
know more about God, I just want to know God more.' But
the more I know about a person, the more I can actually know
that person. The more I know about his character and
accomplishments, the more I'm qualified to praise him. So
let's expand our knowledge of God. After theology lectures
at London Bible College I just wanted to sit and worship, or
stand and shout praise.

We often say that God is all-knowing and present
everywhere, but do we really think about that? God knows
everything all the time. He never has to look in his filing system
for the number of grains of sand or how many hairs on your
head. He knows what Henry VIII was thinking when Anne Boleyn

was beheaded. The universe baffles our minds, but no star slipped into existence while he wasn't looking. He knows, names and numbers them all. And everything was made from nothing! We make things out of matter that already exists. We take paint that is made, brushes we can see and a canvas we can handle. God 'conjured' the universe out of nothing. We're amazed when a conjurer pulls a rabbit out of a hat, but, as R. C. Sproul points out, God started without a rabbit or a hat. He brought the universe into existence out of nothing. That's creativity! (See R. C. Sproul, *The Holiness of God*, Tyndale House.)

God is all-powerful and all-good. Isn't that great? Praise God for his omnipotence! Wouldn't it be terrifying if he were very powerful, but not *totally* powerful? Wouldn't it be dreadful if he *almost* had control of the seasons, the tides and the orbits of suns and moons. Imagine living in a world where God was not quite sovereign. Alternatively, imagine his being totally sovereign but not consistently good. What torture it would be for the universe if God's morality were less than perfect, if he had cruel streaks to his nature, or if he didn't care about right and wrong! We'd feel very insecure if an angel leaked the news, 'God's power will run down in twenty-five years because creating and sustaining the universe has taken so much out of him!'

The reality is, he's eternal, omnipotent, omniscient, good, just, holy, righteous, loving and glorious. What a God we have! The God and Father of our Lord Jesus Christ. Of course we want to praise him. The more we know, the more we appreciate. The more we meditate on him, the more our hearts sing for joy.

Exuberant praise

A true soccer fan is more qualified to praise an excellent move which leads to a magnificent goal. His understanding of the skills involved heightens his enjoyment. But let's add another dimension – identification. A soccer fan can enjoy any goal, but what if *his* team scores? What if *his* son is playing, if it's *his* son who pirouettes, leaves the defence standing and slams the ball into the net leaving the goalkeeper amazed? Now we're talking about ecstatic praise. 'My team! My son! What skill!' What proud father could remain unmoved and offer some polite applause? When Mary was by the empty tomb she didn't note that a resurrection had taken place. She was overwhelmed because her Jesus was alive again.

Quoting C. S. Lewis, Piper says, 'We delight to praise what we enjoy because the praise not merely expresses but completes the enjoyment. It is its appointed consummation. It is not out of compliment that lovers keep on telling one another how beautiful they are. The delight is incomplete until it is expressed.' Piper adds, 'There is the solution. We praise what we enjoy because the delight is incomplete until it is expressed in praise. If we were not allowed to speak of what we value and celebrate, what we love and praise, what we admire, our joy would not be full' (John Piper, *Desiring God*, Multnomah Press, 1986, quoting C. S. Lewis, *Reflections on the Psalms*, Harcourt Brace & World, 1958, pp. 93–95).

Joyfully expressed praise is often followed by admiration and reflection. Outbursts like, 'Well done!' and 'Fantastic!' give way to other sentiments: 'Isn't he wonderful?' or, 'She's amazing.' I can imagine the women who sang, 'David has slain his ten thousands,' reflecting afterwards, 'Isn't he magnificent? I wish I knew him.' So as we fill out our praise we feel a growing longing for God himself and for encounters with him. 'O that You would come to me and manifest Yourself to me.' Suddenly he comes and we feel his nearness, his touch.

> His forever, only His
> Who the Lord and me shall part
> O with what a rest of bliss
> Christ can fill the loving heart
> O to lie forever here

Doubt and care and fear resign
While He whispers in my ear
I am His and He is mine.

One of the most difficult scriptures to read in public is the Song of Solomon. Goodness knows what Eugene Peterson will do with it if he gives it *The Message* treatment! If it's read in public there will probably be a few blushes in the congregation. But why? It's an extraordinary biblical book and has been interpreted in at least two ways.

Throughout the centuries great preachers have seen the Song of Solomon as a poetic description of the love that flows between Christ and his church, the Bridegroom and the bride. Others say that this is unacceptable because the book makes no reference to God and is not interpreted as such in the New Testament. They maintain that the book should be seen simply as a poetic contribution towards man's understanding of romantic love and sexual delight. How amazing that two such different interpretations can come from one book! I don't think that either should be dismissed. Surely we have a love poem and also a description of the relationship between Christ and his church.

We read of love that is better than wine and the desire for deep romance, even passion. The poem starts with enthusiastic longings for closeness, 'Let him kiss me.' Our worship of God leads us into his banqueting house, into his loving heart where we find that our own hearts are almost melted with love for him. Great men and women have written about experiences of overwhelming intimacy with God. David Brainerd wrote, 'I never seemed to be so unhinged from myself and to be so wholly devoted to God. My heart was swallowed up in God most of the day' (Jonathan Edwards (ed.), *Life and Diary of David Brainerd*, Baker Books, 1989). Perhaps this is the heart of all worship, the centre of all God's desire: he's seeking a bride for his Son, one who will love Jesus as he does.

Adam fell into a deep sleep so that a wife could be taken from his side. In the same way our glorious Lord Jesus had his side pierced so that through the blood which flowed could come a justified bride. Jesus' first sign was at a wedding where he created gallons of wine to celebrate the New Covenant. At the end of the Bible we read about the marriage supper of the Lamb to which everything is headed. Our worship will find its ultimate expression in language natural to the love between a bride and groom.

God is seeking worshippers – those who are totally preoccupied with him and who delight themselves in the Lord. They are fascinated by who he is, and they find that their richest experiences are in his presence, either in the great congregation or the secret place. God is seeking lovers who will love him with all their hearts. He is seeking worshippers who will worship him in Spirit and in truth. Are you one of them?

THE CRUCIAL ROLE OF
LEADERSHIP

I f the church is perceived as simply a gathering of people who attend religious services, little leadership is required. Leading the meetings and preaching sermons are all that must be mastered. If, however, the church is seen in a different light, namely as the focal point of God's purposes for world evangelisation and the key centre for discipleship, training, envisioning and releasing ministry, then leadership takes on a totally new meaning.

Leaders are needed who will genuinely inspire a following by their godly character and charismatic gifting. Good leaders are worth their weight in gold. Christians count it a privilege to follow them. The ascended Christ is determined to have a mature and well-functioning church and to accomplish this he gives anointed leadership as top priority. He has ascended on high and has given some to be apostles, some prophets, some evangelists, and some pastors and teachers.

God-given leadership provides security, motivation and direction. A leader who knows he is genuinely called and loved by God brings peace and security to a local church. He gives identity and a sense of destiny to the congregation. He also stirs motivation. God's people are often conscious of their need of motivation. They greatly value a leader who can fan into a flame the fire that can sometimes become dull in their souls. Left to themselves they often feel casual and indifferent, but they can be stirred to enthusiastic action by a charismatic leader.

The vision given to a leader when he is called by God should shape his ministry. Those who follow him will be gripped by his dream and expectation. Such developments are often shown in Scripture. Paul testified that he was not disobedient to the vision impressed on him when God apprehended him. It shaped his life and subsequently the lives of others like Timothy who got caught up in his magnificent obsession. God calls and anoints leaders and then gathers others to their anointing.

Perhaps David's example can serve to illustrate:

> Then all the tribes of Israel came to David at Hebron and said, 'Behold, we are your bone and your flesh. Previously when Saul was king over us, you were the one who led Israel out and in. And the Lord said to you, "You will shepherd My people Israel, and you will be a ruler over Israel."' So all the elders of Israel came to the king at Hebron, and King David made a covenant with them before the Lord at Hebron; then they anointed David king over Israel (2 Sam 5:1–3, NASB).

One of us

In David's anointing for leadership several principles can be observed. First the people said to him, 'We are your bone and your flesh.' It is vital that a true leader is a man of the people, known and loved by them. He is not a stranger or professional outsider.

The kind of mystique associated with some people's concepts of priesthood keeps the 'man of God' away from the people. David was their 'flesh and blood'. Biblical elders were chosen from among the people, not from the distant theological college. Theological study is not to be despised, but wrong concepts of church leadership must be challenged. Too often men have been encouraged to take theological training before they have shown any proof of gifting and calling, and certainly college provides neither.

Charles Simpson tells the following story. He was working at a part-time job when a large, happy, gregarious black lady stopped him as he swept the floor and asked:

> 'You're new around here, ain't you?'
>> 'Yes I am.'
> 'You go to college?' she pressed.
>> 'Yes I do.'
> 'What are you studying?' she asked.
>> 'Well ...' I was not prepared for her examination and my answer must have sounded tentative. 'Well I am studying to be a preacher.'
>
>> She laughed loudly. 'Boy, you don't study to be no preacher. Either you is or you ain't!' (Charles Simpson, *The Challenge to Care*, Vine Books, 1986)

If a man has been called and gifted, however, some training can be of great value. My problem is more with the system that produces an annual crop of ministers from its colleges who are then ordained into their denominations' ministry and thereby regarded as 'ministers'. As such they then 'find a church', arriving as trained professionals. Such ministers initially have no relationship with the churches they are sent to, but are regarded as their leaders.

Leadership doesn't work like this. David's people knew him. He was bone of their bone. In Paul's day elders were appointed from within the flock. Timothy and Titus were not sent from outside by Paul to become church elders, but were to appoint elders from within. The Holy Spirit made overseers from among the flock and they were the church's shepherds (Acts 20).

Those appointing David could say to him, 'Previously when Saul was king over us, you were the one who led Israel out and in' (2 Sam 5:2, NASB). David had shown clear gifting. Even when in a junior position his God-given ability was known by the people who were now about to make him their leader. He was no stranger to them; he did not come with mere paper qualifications. When Paul laid hands on elders in the New Testament churches, or when he sent Titus or Timothy to take their responsibility on his behalf, he would appoint known and gifted men.

Some modern denominations have a policy of moving their ministers from place to place with great speed so that they never form relationships with their people. I was once addressing a large ministers' conference in South Africa and the leader of the denomination told me he moved ministers from church to church every two or three years. When asked why, he explained that they would have given all they had to give after two or three years. No time was given to forming relationships, so the pastors became the loneliest people in the church (except for their wives, who were often lonelier ...).

How can we build loving communities of deeply integrated people if the leader himself is a stranger in our midst? His appeal to people on the edges of the church to become more involved can sound rather hollow when everybody knows that he, the pastor, is the biggest 'outsider' in the place. He knows nobody and nobody knows him beyond the extent of his professional pastoral relationships with them.

His calling

Next, those appointing David made reference to his own personal calling. They knew that God had said to him, 'You will shepherd My people Israel.' They had confidence he was God's man living under the influence of God's personal call. He would not be simply a man-made appointment with a man-pleasing agenda. He had promises from God burning in his heart; he had a secret experience with God; he had the powerful Samuel anointing in his history. Now he was coming to true spiritual government with a deep sense of commissioning in his soul.

No man can take spiritual leadership to himself. If he is not called and commissioned by God, why should anybody follow him? But if he is, he needs freedom to lead from the front. Democratic structures, committees and boards represent a totally different form of church leadership – one which is unknown in the Bible. Anointing and calling are God's way of maintaining his government in his church. Christ ascended on high. He gave gifts of leadership.

Israel succeeded as a nation when it was led by called and anointed leaders. Charismatic leadership is God's gift to the church. He chooses whom he anoints with gifts of leadership so he retains his rule. When God anoints someone, his anointing becomes apparent to all. The spiritual gifting that is demonstrated as a result of the anointing gives public profile to the individual concerned. Often gifting in preaching or communicating the word begins to demonstrate God's hand upon a man. This gives him a sphere of influence, and people begin to realise that they hear God through this man – he seems to bring God nearer to them. If his character and leadership skills match this public skill in the word of God, people begin to gather to him for spiritual leadership. This is a spiritual development, not an institutional one. As his vision, leadership skills and ability to communicate bear fruit in lives, he begins to have a God-given sphere of influence. People become joined to him like people did to David. They begin to speak as those said to David, 'We are yours, O David.'

Some Christians become nervous at this point, uneasy about the personal nature of this commitment, but God builds churches by joining people together in love and trust and personal loyalty, as well as individual devotion to Jesus. Paul testified, 'They gave themselves first to the Lord and then to us' (2 Cor 8:5). When men gave themselves to David the Bible does not see this as a mistake or a fleshly rush of enthusiasm. In fact it records the statement was made by men upon whom the Holy Spirit had come and inspired their spoken commitment (1 Chron 12:18). David in turn received them and appointed them to positions of authority according to their gifting. Thus God's anointing on David was the prevailing factor in the forming of the people. David was anointed to lead; others responded to that gifting and yielded themselves to its influence. The men who did this were not weaklings or 'yes men'; the Bible makes it plain that they were powerful in their own right. Their exploits were legendary, their courage was clear for all to see. These tough fearless individuals found great joy in submitting their lives to David's God-given leadership skill, so that they too could enjoy the benefits of the prophetic promises that shaped David's life.

A God-given sphere

Next, notice that David ruled in a God-given sphere – God had called him to rule over Israel. His sphere was the whole nation. That was God's calling upon him, he did not snatch it. Indeed he had waited patiently throughout Saul's rule, but now he entered into what God had planned for him. Now by God's will he was to lead Israel.

The New Testament church was told, 'Obey your leaders' (Heb 13:17); 'Respect those who ... are over you in the Lord' (1 Thess 5:12). These spiritual principles of leadership must be in place. It is difficult to apply these principles in an institutional situation. If a leader is simply a denominational appointment and shows none of the leadership characteristics described in the Bible, it is very difficult to say, 'We are yours.' If the man lacks calling, anointing, vision and motivation, nothing stirs you inwardly to express your commitment. Loyalty has to be inspired and earned.

Institutional Christianity does not produce this kind of chemistry. One British national newspaper described a minister as 'a general dog's body looking after a group of well-meaning but harmless people'. Obviously this is not always the case, but it is often the way our media portray things and it sometimes feels like the truth.

Laying on of hands

Finally in the account of David's appointment comes the actual covenant between ruler and people and the further anointing to fulfil the ministry. Thus in the New Testament all preparation leads up to actual laying on of hands for recognised responsibility. Surely at this point further anointing is given to the publicly recognised shepherd of the flock and the people are publicly acknowledging their willing desire for him to lead them.

New Testament elders are always referred to in plural. The anointed leader of a work does not stand alone but as an elder among elders. In a small work plurality might prove impossible. It may be that only one so far shows evidence of God's anointing on him. We should not rush into laying hands on anyone suddenly (1 Tim 5:22) simply to make up numbers and prove we are biblical, but we must expect the biblical norm of plurality to emerge. No one should be co-opted when there is no proof of gifting or calling. Appointments without gifting will soon lead the church into a cold institution. If a man is not called or gifted but holds office, he is simply an appointment, and we begin to drift away from biblical norms into religious externality.

Those appointed by God into positions of leadership in the church have a high calling. They not only teach the word and lead the people, they also set the tone of the church. They create its atmosphere and style and establish its philosophy of ministry. Their own sense of calling and destiny provides security, motivation and direction to the church. It is, therefore, difficult to overstate the key role of leadership and its charismatic nature.

We should not be surprised to note a great contrast between churches led by genuine, anointed leaders who are loved, valued, respected and given freedom to lead, and churches where democracy rules. Boards and committees, elections and voting are unknown in Scripture. There must come a rediscovery of biblical norms where the Holy Spirit calls and equips leadership and where that leadership is given room to operate.

Prayerful brainstorming

This does not mean that times of prayerful brainstorming and discussion are inappropriate. In Acts 15 we see a time of tension in the early church over the matter of circumcision. It was resolved through discussion and godly interaction. In conclusion the elders and apostles present were able to send a message to all the churches which represented their united decision. They said, 'It seemed good to the Holy Spirit and to us' (Acts 15:28).

Several men shared their perspectives. Scriptures were quoted, examples from their previous experience were noted. Finally James spoke with an authority which satisfied all who were present and his perspective was happily owned by everybody. In all of this their preoccupation was to ensure that they were genuinely obeying the Holy Spirit and not simply seeing what the majority felt. They were deeply conscious that they were serving God in his church and that the Holy Spirit was among them to lead.

As a young Christian I was invited to become a member of my local Baptist church. I had been blessed and built up there through the faithful teaching of the godly pastor. Having attended for a few years and been baptised, I was told that if I became a member, I could attend the church business meetings and even vote on issues and decisions facing the church.

As a comparatively inexperienced believer I followed the advice given, but I can only say that when I actually attended the 'business meeting' I was profoundly shocked by its atmosphere. It was vastly different from the Sunday services where the pastor's God-given skills and obvious spiritual authority enriched all who were present. Here, he was addressed as an employee with no more authority than anyone else. Angry people 'proposed', others 'seconded'. Hands and voices were raised, not in worship and acknowledgement of the Holy Spirit's presence, but in an endeavour to make sure that personal preferences were heard. Prayer had been a formal preliminary. This, it seems, was democracy at work. As a spiritually unqualified young believer I could have my vote and it had as much authority as that of the pastor who had served the church for years. I was dismayed!

Where tradition is the entrenched norm, and democratic power is held by a majority who treasure the past, we should not be surprised to note little freedom of movement or spiritual progress. When the Holy Spirit says, 'Behold, I do a new thing,' sadly the democratic vote will often reply, 'Not here you won't.'

SPIRITUAL AUTHORITY

S piritual authority. The words send a shiver down many a Christian spine! Yet when correctly handled true spiritual authority creates security, peace and real joy in the Holy Spirit. Everything depends upon how it is handled.

The only time that Jesus particularly pointed out to his disciples that he was their Master and Lord was as he disrobed, took a towel and, as a servant, washed their feet. He did it as an example, a visual aid. It would be for ever inscribed upon their memories. Many years later, Peter was writing to elders and reminding them to be examples and not to lord it over the flock. 'Clothe yourselves with humility,' he continued, doubtless reflecting on that unforgettable night.

Jesus contrasted his kingdom with the world when he said, 'You know that the rulers of the Gentiles lord it over them, and their high officials exercise authority over them. Not so with you. Instead, whoever wants to become great among you must be your servant' (Mt 20:25–26).

The restoration of spiritual authority opens a way fraught with dangers. How easy to take hold of verses and drive them to false conclusions! How easy to lust for positions of prestige and power where authority can be exercised! How easy to miss totally the Spirit of Christ! There are real dangers and there have undoubtedly been abuses, but this must not drive us away from God-given principles. Leaders must have freedom to lead the church, or we shall never advance.

Close inspection reveals what style that leadership should adopt. Writing to the Thessalonians, Paul said, 'We were gentle among you, like a mother caring for her little children ... as a father deals with his own children' (1 Thess 2:7, 11). He addressed the Philippians, 'My brothers, you whom I love and long for' (Phil 4:1). And to the Corinthians he said, 'I am not writing this to shame you, but to warn you, as my dear children' (1 Cor 4:14). Nursing mother, father, brothers, children – they are all intimate family terms.

Meekness and gentleness

When the apostle spoke to the churches, he was led by 'the meekness and gentleness of Christ' (2 Cor 10:1). Although he used strong language in very serious situations, he more often implored the believers to hear him and encouraged others to adopt this same loving attitude. 'If someone is caught in a sin, you who are spiritual should restore him gently' (Gal 6:1) he said, and advocated the same spirit of gentleness towards those who opposed sound teaching (2 Tim 2:24–25).

Paul did not order the Corinthians, 'Do this!' Rather, he appealed to their wisdom: 'I speak to sensible people; judge for yourselves what I say' (1 Cor 10:15). He did not bully the weak, but became weak in order to win them (1 Cor 9:22). This is the spirit of Christ in operation and God longs to see it motivating his church.

The fact is that spiritual authority only operates properly where people have happily yielded themselves to it. It cannot be forced upon the unwilling. Hearts must first be won and trust be gained. We have seen that the men who joined David's growing army said, 'We are yours.' These new recruits had come to love and respect David. They wholeheartedly gave him their allegiance. David did not have to argue for his authority but could rest in the fact that, not unlike Jesus, all that the Father had given him would come to him.

A man who often contends for his own authority is actually betraying the fact that he is insecure in that role.

A time to correct

Confrontation is an important responsibility for all church leaders since it guards the flock of God against error. If, however, correction is more frequent than encouragement, people have great difficulty receiving it. God wants his shepherds to relate to the flock as friends. When people know they are loved, they will often receive words that will hurt, because they believe that 'faithful are the wounds of a friend' (Prov 27:6, NASB).

Correction must be done with love. A surgeon has one goal: to make his patient well again. However, he knows that there is a right time and place for the operation – he doesn't lop something off as he passes his patient in the corridor – and he knows that he must prepare himself – he doesn't turn up drunk and disorderly at the operating theatre!

If there is a problem with someone in the church, we do not put the matter off for two years, but neither do we say, 'It's about time I spoke to him,' and plunge in the knife! We react in a spirit of gentleness: 'This is a delicate operation. I've got to prepare myself and pray for the right moment and setting. God, help me to express love.'

Building up

The purpose of all spiritual authority is to bless and build up the flock of God. It should be the outworking of the love and devotion of the leadership to the people. There should grow a developing expression of love. Paul said to the Corinthians that they did not have many fathers. God is looking for fatherly love from leadership towards the flock.

One of the goals of parents is to create within their children the ability to make wise decisions. Sadly, some parents fail at this because they dominate their children. They give commands instead of counsel, orders instead of training and scolding instead of correction, thereby producing insecurity and low self-worth in their offspring. Church leaders must avoid the same dangers.

Jesus said, 'The kings of the Gentiles lord it over them ... But you are not to be like that' (Lk 22:25–26). The leader who dominates will become suspicious of the people, particularly when they come up with new ideas. 'Jim's got another wonderful plan for the worship meeting!' the leader will grumble, and feel threatened. Creative thinkers can be regarded as enemies. In time, the leader will communicate to the people, 'We don't want anyone here to think, thank you,' frustrating those who have a valuable contribution to make. A possessive attitude in a leader will stifle people's genuine expression of loyalty and make them suspicious. Leaders must not fear the people and prevent them from offering their contributions. I am only too ready to admit that some of the best things we have developed in New Frontiers International have not come from my personal initiatives. And some of the major changes at Church of Christ the King in Brighton have come about in response to prophecies that other people have given. We can all hear and contribute.

Spiritual authority does not eradicate the wisdom of the body but draws on it. Paul says, 'Not that we lord it over your faith, but we work with you for your joy' (2 Cor 1:24). Leaders are there not to dominate others' faith, but to help them to be joyful and fulfilled. Leaders do not force people to recognise their spiritual authority. They lead by example. Paul did not say to Timothy, 'Let no man despise your youth – show them who's boss!' Instead, he exhorted him to set an example to the believers 'in life, in love, in faith and in purity' (1 Tim 4:12).

A peaceful conscience

Paul said, 'We commend ourselves to every man's conscience in the sight of God' (2 Cor 4:2). Leaders can be knowledgeable and eloquent, but if they cannot commend themselves to people's consciences they will not be followed. People want leaders whom they know to be godly, trustworthy and transparent. If leaders do commend themselves to their people's conscience, then, in spite of their weakness and vulnerability, they will find their people following happily.

If a leader's character must appeal to people's conscience, so must his words. A young man told me that his pastor had said to him, 'I believe that you should move closer to the church and that your wife should give up her job to look after the children.' The young man asked me, 'If we don't do these things, are we disobeying God?'

'No,' I replied. 'If you do something just because you are told to, you are not combining your action with faith. If, in a few weeks' time, you find yourself in debt, you will blame your pastor. Leadership cannot force its will. This man has brought you his counsel and now he wants you to pray about it. If his advice witnesses with your conscience, God will give you faith for it. Only when you are convinced that God has told you to do something can you commit yourself to it with faith. You must give full weight to your pastor's counsel, but you must also arrive at your own faith.'

This same principle can work in another way. A church member may come to the leadership and say, 'God is calling me to the mission field and I want to join "X" missionary society.' But the group of leaders may feel uneasy and advise him not to proceed. So now what happens? Does this mean he is forbidden to advance? Is he a rebel if he ignores counsel?

No. Leaders must appeal to the individual's conscience, to his walk with God. They must say, 'We do not have faith for this. We cannot go beyond our conscience, but neither can we force our will on you.'

If he is then accepted by the missionary society, he must be free to proceed, but he in turn must not expect the leaders of the church publicly to lay hands upon him and send him, for he has proceeded on his own initiative. Leaders must not feel obliged to lay hands on all who feel that they are called to the mission field. Leaders can still express their love and care to the intended missionary, but they must not go beyond their own faith by laying hands upon him if they doubt his call. In the end, time will prove who was right. This procedure can be followed with genuine openness of heart and love.

Room to breathe

Spiritual authority must leave room to breathe and must never dominate people's lives. Once leaders have offered their counsel, they must give people space – the chance to find out for themselves what God is saying.

God may do the most extraordinary things through certain individuals, even when they seem to break every rule in the book! But there will still be those who return in six months and say, 'I'm sorry. I got it wrong. I didn't listen.' If this happens they don't need to be treated like rebels. Rather, the church should reaffirm their love for them and joyfully welcome them back.

If the leadership holds things too tightly, the church will never make the extraordinary and spontaneous breakthroughs that seem to characterise the book of Acts. There we see Philip suddenly going to the Samaritans, Peter amazingly going to Cornelius' home without first checking with the other apostles, and Ananias going to see the hated and feared Saul just because the Spirit told him to go. Some of the most amazing advances in the book of Acts come when individuals respond to the personal promptings of the Holy Spirit. They are not the result of cleverly strategised movements coming from spiritual leadership.

In reality any sensitive member of the body of Christ can hear the Holy Spirit and respond to his promptings.

Willing to be accountable

It is important to notice, however, that Philip was more than willing to give account for his work in Samaria to Peter and John when they came from Jerusalem to see what God was doing through his ministry there. Philip did not withstand their enquiries, insisting that this was *his* sphere of service. Rather, he allowed Peter and John to bring their apostolic wisdom to his evangelistic initiative.

Also, Peter was willing to answer the enquiries of the other apostles when they asked questions about his going to the Gentile Cornelius. He did not simply argue that he as an individual had full freedom to do whatever he liked. He was more than willing, having obeyed the Holy Spirit, to then work out his accountability to the other apostles by making full explanation of why he had gone to a Gentile home and baptised Gentiles.

In the early church there was freedom to respond to individual promptings of the Holy Spirit, but also a genuine sense of accountability and spiritual authority, so the mighty New Testament church moved on in power and security.

God has given spiritual authority for our safety and protection. There is plenty of room for diversity of gift, but God wants us to be united in spirit and to know those who are over us in the Lord. The goal of every church leader is to produce mature, outgoing, well-relating people who can cope with pressure and build secure relationships. The leader's goal is like Paul's, namely to present everyone mature, not everyone dependent.

In reality, a truly mature person does not withstand the counsel of others. Aware of his own limitations and blind spots, he is grateful to God for those who love him sufficiently to bring him counsel and admonition. He will be aware that he can be misled and ensnared by the devil and so will be grateful for the checks and balances which spiritual authority provides.

Do you enjoy the benefits of accountability to someone in the body of Christ? Do you know and appreciate those who are over you in the Lord (1 Thess 5:12)?

Beware the dangers of the 'lone ranger' mentality – well-intentioned, perhaps, but answerable to no one. Find your place in a local church and develop relationships with responsible leadership so that you can grow and be helped towards Christian maturity.

You will learn to give thanks for God's gift of spiritual authority.

HUMILITY MAKES
CHANGE POSSIBLE

W inston Churchill once described a political opponent as a 'humble man', adding caustically, 'But then he has much to be humble about.' Churchill's acid wit seems to suggest that humility is an admirable quality only when groundless. Humility displayed by the unimpressive is no virtue, whereas it is to be admired in the gifted and able.

When Paul urged the Ephesian Christians to act with all humility, he used a word which no Greek would have admired. The Greeks despised humility and dismissed the weak as irrelevant. Greek culture applauded aggression and drive. When Jesus said, 'The meek shall inherit the earth,' he totally baffled human expectations. Surely the powerful will inherit everything? Surely the well-connected, the resourceful, the politically strong, are the ones to be envied? Not so – humility holds the prize. Meekness inherits. Now if humility is only authentic when it is groundless, is there a trick? Are we all being called upon to kid ourselves? And does it matter anyway?

Make no mistake, humility must be cultivated as a lifestyle if we are to succeed in our mission to build effective local churches. Jesus invites us to learn from him and adds, 'I am meek and lowly of heart.' Few of us bring genuine humility with us when we are first saved. Our experience of conversion may have been our first taste of real lowliness of heart – when we suddenly realised we were unworthy and could not save ourselves.

We needed forgiveness. We became conscious of our need. But the tragic thing is that many Christians seem to move on from their early sense of vulnerability, quickly recover their self-esteem and lurch back into pride and complacency.

Simon Peter was humbled to the dust after Jesus had borrowed his boat, preached and then filled his net with fish. 'Depart from me. I am a sinful man,' was his reaction. To follow Jesus and become a fisher of men was a huge privilege. How could he, unworthy as he was, be invited to spend his days with Christ? As time went by, however, another attitude emerged. 'They were not with us, so we forbade them.' 'They may deny you, but I never will.' Party spirit, self-sufficiency and pride replaced his former humility as Peter became a candidate for total collapse and bitter regret. His experience stands as the classic illustration of the God-given proverb that pride comes before a fall.

How then are we to understand and maintain true humility? First, it is not a religious façade. Not 'play-acting' as we stand back at every door and insist 'after you'. It is no mere cosmetic, covering the cracks of our true feelings. The roots of genuine humility go very deep. They feed on the fact of who we are in the light of God and our call to walk worthy of him.

Potter and clay

God is the all-powerful Creator. We are mere creatures. This is the first ground for humility. This must not be forgotten by a generation of Christians surrounded by atheists and evolutionists who have abandoned all respect for a Creator. Society does not consider the claims of a Creator. While modern man concerns himself with women's rights, gay rights and everybody else's rights, he has no thought for the right of a Creator that we should fear and honour him. Scriptures which describe him as the Potter and us as the clay are far from their thinking.

Humility is appropriate for pots. Honour is appropriate for the potter! On the basis of creatureliness alone we should remain humble. But we are not only pots – we are rebel pots! Wilful sinners, we have ignored our Creator and his requirements and chosen our way. Now our only hope before a holy God is that he have mercy on us. We are not only creatures; by our sinful nature we are disqualified creatures. The fact that God is willing to show us mercy and draw us back to himself, not only as forgiven sinners but also as totally accepted, vindicated and valued sons, should overwhelm us with humility for the rest of our days. To think that God delights in a rebel sinner like me is absolutely fantastic. To know that he has qualified me to inherit his glory as a beloved son is totally staggering.

We should also be humbled by the fact that God speaks to us at all. Why should the glorious, holy, all-knowing Creator God speak to ignorant sinners like us? Our minds have been darkened. Our understanding has become limited and marred by sin and its devastating results. With regard to true realities we have become fools, yet God speaks to us. Why should he bother?

'I talk to the trees,' says the old romantic song; 'that's why they put me away,' adds the cynical Spike Milligan parody. Only fools talk to trees. Some talk to their dogs and their plants, assuring us that every word is understood.

The reality is that most of us only talk to those who can understand. We don't waste our words on inanimate objects or canine friends whose limitations are plain for all to see. I must confess that when pet owners tell me, 'He understands every word I say to him,' I long to ask what Fido's view is of the difficulties facing the government as it contemplates the present economic climate. Of course pets don't understand! God has not equipped them to. Yet wonder of wonders, we sinful creatures, with all our limitations, are spoken to by the living God! He calls us into fellowship with himself. Was anything so humbling as this?

Meekness or weakness?

Humility is appropriate for mere mortals. Lowliness is essential for the elect. But how is it expressed? Are we all to become Uriah

Heeps? Is our testimony to become, 'I am a mere nothing'? Not at all! Beware the pendulum swing from self-sufficiency and pride to self-despising and even self-denial. Healthy humility does not undermine our personhood and leave us devastated and irrelevant. It is simply an appropriate stance for redeemed human beings with a glorious future before them. True humility does not destroy our identity but prepares us for future glory and fulfilment beyond our wildest dreams. God doesn't want to eliminate us. He wants us to inherit the kingdom!

Caleb was a truly humble man. While everyone else questioned Moses' spiritual authority and claimed their right to express an opinion, Caleb was an exception. He spoke of Moses with awed respect. He honoured him as 'the servant of the Lord' and 'the man of God'. His humility was exposed.

Did this turn him into a pushover, a lifeless wimp? Was this meek and lowly man easily dismissed by his macho contemporaries who challenged Moses without fear? Not at all. The lowly Caleb demonstrated a manliness and courage which shamed his colleagues. 'Give me this mountain,' he appealed as he prepared himself for warfare. The arrogant who had challenged Moses' right to lead them were long since dead in the wilderness. The meek Caleb inherited the earth!

Pride is a snare. Self-sufficiency is an illusion. It robs us of so much. The proud of Jesus' day totally disqualified themselves from what God was so willing to give. Proclaiming themselves 'Abraham's sons', they felt no need of further light or freedom. Claiming that they were never in bondage, they forfeited the liberty that Jesus came to give.

Beware of pride

Pride and prejudice are powerful enemies of spiritual advance. How many times have you missed a blessing from God because the channel of blessing that God had raised up was not from your group? Many arrogantly dismissed the so-called 'Wimber wobbles' and thereby missed the refreshing touch of the Holy Spirit that came through that choice servant of God. Attacking the so-called 'faith movement', others found their refuge in unbelief and cynicism. Pride is a thief.

It is also a killer! It stops you taking risks. What about your reputation? What will people think of you if you make a mistake? You may be ridiculed. You may look a fool. You don't want to appear childish. How many well-taught and safe Evangelicals have refused to risk a fresh move of the Holy Spirit? Forgetting the clear teaching of Jesus that we must become as a little child to inherit the kingdom, we wrap ourselves around with our garments of superior knowledge and years of experience. Muttering cynically, we take our refuge in caution and criticism. Pride takes many forms and guises.

When we are young and earnest we are open to receiving many new things. As we grow older we gather certain safeguards. We have learned much. Maybe we have earned the respect of others. Why jeopardise it all by becoming vulnerable again? So we imitate the sins of the Pharisees of Jesus' day. Dismissing the disciples of Christ as unlearned men, they refused to enter the kingdom of God. Claiming knowledge and undeniable religious pedigree, they failed to humble themselves. They tripped over the stone of stumbling that Jesus and his followers represented, because they were arrogant and self-sufficient.

A vital clue was provided by the apostle Paul when he asked the ensnared Corinthians, 'What do you have that you were not given?' Where is room for pride? He went on to assure them, 'All things are yours.' There are no limitations to what God is willing to give, but he will give to the hungry and thirsty and will satisfy the humble. How terrifying to be opposed by God. How glorious to be given more grace.

When is humility most tested? One of the most searching tests is when you are falsely accused – especially when your personal motives are challenged. The urge to defend yourself and plead innocence can be very great. Jesus said that you are blessed when people insult you and falsely say all kinds of evil against you for his sake. He added that you are to rejoice and be glad! Easier said than done!

Paul discovered a wonderful key when he said, 'I care very little if I am judged by you or by any human court' (1 Cor 4:3). Caring little about other people's judgement of you is glorious liberty. I don't care too much about what some people think of me, but there are many whose opinions I value highly. Paul found freedom from caring about other people's views of him by caring even more about God's view. He was willing to leave things with God, who 'will bring to light what is hidden in darkness and will expose the motives of men's hearts. At that time each will receive his praise from God' (1 Cor 4:5). A day is coming when all secrets will be revealed; not only secret actions, but cunningly concealed motives.

What a day that will be! Your heart will be an open book for all to read. If you have never had a humbling experience before, you can be sure that one is coming! One of Paul's keys to genuine humility was to keep that day always before him. It was an attitude rooted in reality. A day of total exposure and accountability lies before us. The Lord himself will be the Judge. Why should I be preoccupied with any other opinion?

Powerful praise

If being unfairly attacked constitutes the greatest test to humility, being praised must be in there fighting for second place. Handling applause and commendation can be heady stuff. Some have stood through the severe winters of bitter and unrighteous opposition only to stumble and fall in the melting heat of popularity and praise.

The disciples must have been thrilled when Jesus not only drew the Jewish crowds but attracted even the Greeks. Andrew and Philip were no doubt excited as they came to tell Jesus the news. International acclaim awaited them! But what a response

Jesus gave! 'Unless a grain of wheat falls to the ground and dies, it remains only a single seed. But if it dies, it produces many seeds. The man who loves his life will lose it, while the man who hates his life in this world will keep it for eternal life' (Jn 12:24–25).

Jesus, as our forerunner, humbled himself and was obedient to death. We must have his mind in us. Following our meek and lowly King, we must work out our salvation, assured that he is working in us. Doing everything without complaining or arguing, we must humbly prove ourselves pure and blameless – children of God in an arrogant and depraved generation. This attitude is so foreign among fallen humanity that we shall shine like stars in the universe (Phil 2:3–16).

So the humble will shine like stars and the meek will inherit the earth. These upside-down values will encircle the globe in the end-time kingdom until once again we hear the cry associated with the early church, 'These men who are turning the world upside down have come here also.'

Will you humble yourself, not in empty pious prayers and phrases, but in costly decisions that might make you feel awkward and vulnerable? Will you cast yourself only on the faithfulness of God and his declared commitment to give grace to the humble and in due season exalt them?

Massive changes have undoubtedly got to take place in local churches if they are to become relevant to this generation and to be sufficiently flexible wineskins for the Holy Spirit's activity. If we refuse to change our style and cling tenaciously to the past with our familiar and comfortable patterns, we must not be surprised if more relevant and flexible churches spring up all around us which gather thirsty people searching for a God who is accessible to the modern culture. The true gospel will always retain its own offence. The local church does not need to add more offence by being out of date and unyielding. It takes humility to acknowledge the need to change. It takes more humility to accept each uncomfortable and maybe costly step as it comes.

It takes a very humble church to acknowledge that maybe it is building on the wrong foundation altogether. Perhaps it needs to open itself to a prophetic ministry to speak into its situation and bring an objective assessment. Many modern businesses that want to succeed invite management consultants to investigate their operation. By doing so they are acknowledging their own limitations and demonstrating openness to change. The local church, shut in on itself with no exposure to the fresh breeze of a prophetic challenge, can become a stagnant pool without realising it. The church should be God's prophetic voice to the world, but to speak for God we must first hear from God.

In the New Testament, travelling prophetic ministries helped to keep local churches on course and remain true to the essentially prophetic nature of the church in the world, and to this we now turn.

A PROPHETIC PEOPLE

I wonder what comes to your mind when you hear the phrase 'a prophetic people'? Maybe you imagine a dishevelled line of individuals, clad in camel-hair garments and patiently waiting for their daily ration of locusts and wild honey!

Flowing beards and far-away looks seem to be fundamental to the role, so how can we modern sophisticates go to work from Monday to Friday in our cars and trains in collars and ties and be a prophetic people? How can housewives who take their children to the school gates sound a prophetic note?

Old Testament roots

First of all we need to understand that the earliest prophets, like us, were actually people of their age. Abraham, for instance (the first person actually called a prophet in the Bible), was wealthy and lived in a sophisticated city. He had family and friends, flocks and servants. He was no mystic. Nevertheless, he heard from God and saw a vision which transformed and dominated his life.

He developed a relationship of amazing intimacy with Yahweh, and gained the title 'the friend of God' (2 Chron 20:7). Before judging Sodom and Gomorrah the question arose in heaven, 'Shall I hide from Abraham what I am about to do?' (Gen 18:17). This led to a prolonged conversation between God and Abraham concerning that very judgement, thereby underlining the word of Amos that 'the Sovereign Lord does nothing without revealing his plan to his servants the prophets' (Amos 3:7).

Abraham was taken up with God's plans, not with his own sense of personal fulfilment. As he embraced these plans wholeheartedly Abraham found his life's destiny and purpose. He was not on a 'bless me' trip, even though God did bless him and made him a blessing to the nations. Without prophetic goals we tend to see God as existing simply to meet our needs. Even Abraham's spiritual development and growth in holiness were not essentially a personal and private matter. They were hammered out on the anvil of God's programme for the blessing of the world.

Following Abraham, the prophetic stream flowed on through Isaac, Jacob and particularly Joseph, whose whole life story reflected God's purpose for his people. Joseph saw visions, but these were no mere charismatic experiences. The rest of his life was a vindication and proof of their reality and relevance.

After Joseph, God raised up Moses, who is perhaps the Old Testament's most outstanding prophet. When he was a child his mother sowed the seeds of prophetic vision in his mind and heart. This meant that, although Egypt gave him education and wealth, he considered the reproach of association with God's prophetic people to be of far greater value. God's ultimate intention for his people mastered him and motivated his decisions. Later, a true prophetic call gripped his life so that 'the Lord used a prophet to bring Israel up from Egypt, and by a prophet he cared for him' (Hos 12:13). The short-sighted and reluctant Israelites ultimately arrived at their destination through Moses' faithfulness to his prophetic call.

Next, the prophet Samuel introduced a new 'kingdom age'. The nation was familiar with prophets and priests, but they had never before been led by a king. Tragically many subsequent priests and kings drifted away from God and even some of the prophets proved false. The true prophet was always in demand. Before the Israelites went into exile, the prophets called them to repent and return to God. In captivity Ezekiel outlined how the people should live. Jeremiah had informed them that they would return to the Promised Land, and to Daniel was given the privilege of seeing what would happen in the future. When the Israelites did begin to return to their land, Haggai and Zechariah encouraged them in the building programme. Jonah challenged their narrowness, and Jeremiah and Ezekiel raised their sights to a new promised covenant.

The new dispensation

Not only did John the Baptist prepare the way for Jesus, he also declared, 'He will baptise you with the Holy Spirit and with fire' (Lk 3:16). John was heralding a new day of the Spirit. Instead of being given only to individuals, the Spirit would soon be available to everyone.

What John the Baptist foretold, the apostle Peter confirmed. Taking the words of the prophet Joel, Peter applied them to the Day of Pentecost. 'This is it!' he told the people who had gathered to see what was happening. 'The new age has arrived! Sons, daughters, young and old will prophesy, see visions and dream dreams. The Holy Spirit is now being poured out on all of God's servants.'

The Old Testament prophets longed to understand what God would do in the last days, but they were denied that privilege (1 Pet 1:10). Now, however, in this new dispensation the apostle Paul tells us that the mystery has been fully revealed by the Spirit to God's holy apostles and prophets in a way that it had not been in previous generations (Eph 3:5). The prophetic ministry therefore continues in the church (Eph 4:11).

The Bible tells us that we are built on the foundation of the apostles and prophets (Eph 2:20). There are two ways in which we can understand this. First, the apostles and prophets laid the foundation at the beginning of the church age and the church is universally and historically built on it. Secondly, every local church needs to make sure that it is also built on the same apostolic and prophetic foundation. A foundation is a crucial part of a building, though it is later hidden from sight when the structure is completed. What is laid foundationally determines the future shape, size and potential of the building.

Paul wanted to preach where Christ was not known so that he would not be building on someone else's foundation (Rom 15:20). In addition, in 1 Corinthians 3:10, Paul pointed out that as a wise master builder he 'laid a foundation' in the Corinthian church. Laying a foundation in a local church was a dynamic concept which Paul regarded as part of his ministry. He did not want to build on 'another man's foundation'.

Some time ago I asked a surveyor if I could build a room above my garage. To my surprise, instead of focusing on the appropriate space above the garage, his eyes were fixed on the slab of concrete on which the garage stood. When I told him that I did not want a basement, he laughed and told me that the foundation would determine whether or not I could extend above the existing building. I could not. The foundation was inadequate.

Modern churches are built on all sorts of foundations. Some are built on tradition, some on institution, and some on democracy or sentimentality. In many local churches biblical practices like speaking in tongues are forbidden, because they are foreign to the particular tradition. 'You cannot build that here. The foundations will not take it.' Radical plans to change the programme can meet with hostility, because people are sentimentally attached to 'the way we've always done it here'. The unwieldy 'majority church vote' can successfully keep such a church rooted in a bygone century. Send a prophet to speak to it and he will be 'stoned'.

Churches are sometimes built on a predominantly pastoral gift. When this is the case, they run the risk of concentrating on the needs of the flock rather than on the purpose of God! The flock can come to see pastoral care as the key factor of church life. The church can be constantly evaluated on the basis of whether its personal needs are being met rather than on whether God's purpose is being fulfilled. For instance, pragmatic changes that should be made in the church programme can be withstood because of undue consideration being given to any discomfort the congregation might face. Thus necessary cell subdivisions or multiple services might be resisted by a church simply because people express their personal preferences instead of embracing God's guidance for incorporating growth.

If a church is built essentially and exclusively on a teaching gift, it will tend to produce a preaching centre that gathers a crowd but does not build a body. If the major leadership role is in the hands of an evangelist, the local church will reflect the immediacy of his burden for the lost, but again it will not build all that God wants for the local church.

The New Testament teaches that a church will succeed when the vital ministries of pastor, teacher and evangelist are built on an apostolic/prophetic foundation. Without exposure to a prophet, a whole congregation may be Spirit-filled and speaking in tongues, but not know why. Even good churches, if they are not caught up with God's ultimate intention, will find themselves becoming parochial and stagnating instead of reaching the world. The prophet insists on reminding us of our true identity and our calling to make disciples of all the nations. He will not allow us to settle as an inward-looking group.

In our early days as a church in Brighton, prophetic foundations were laid, helping us to understand something of our future calling and significance. God promised us, through prophecy, that he had set before us an open door. He also promised us a certain level of visibility that would make us a blessing to the whole town. Years later, when we tried to buy an industrial building and transform it into a worship centre, we were opposed unanimously by the local council. We were also told that perhaps a council decision reached by a small majority of, say, 60% against and 40% for the project might be overturned by an appeal. The reversal of an 80% to 20% decision was extremely rare. A 100%

refusal was regarded as virtually impossible to change by appeal. We prayed, we appealed, we believed the prophetic promise and we enjoyed the victory which the Lord Jesus gave us as the door swung open and we bought and transformed the building in which we now worship.

God also told us that we would see young people come up through our ranks who would be trained and sent to the nations. Having grown up like shoots among us, he would cut them and fire them out like arrows.

These prophetic utterances have shaped our expectations and church life. We know who we are and what we are called to do. When in Africa recently I spent time with one of the young men formerly with us as a student in Brighton, now leading a church in Ghana. He planted it using insights he had gained while with us, and continues enjoying our involvement with him as the church there grows and develops.

Prophetic roots

When Jeremiah and Ezekiel tried to bring the nation of Israel back to their prophetic roots, they were regarded as enemies of the people. They could not bless what God was not blessing. God is prepared to shake and tear down everything which dishonours him. He is prepared for the Temple to be destroyed, for the Ark to be stolen, for a television evangelist to be exposed, for his holy name to be dragged through the mud. But he is committed to raising a pure prophetic people who will follow him wholeheartedly.

Jeremiah prophesied that after seventy years the Israelites would return to the Promised Land. The story of Ezra begins, '... in order to fulfil the word of the Lord spoken by Jeremiah ...' The nation's recovery programme was rooted in the prophetic word. A new day had dawned! When Haggai later rebuked the people for concentrating more on building their own homes than the Lord's house, he was speaking relevantly into their situation.

They had responded to Jeremiah's prophecy and, since Haggai was building on that foundation, they immediately responded to his reproof.

Churches whose existence and identity have been affected by prophetic foundations can appreciate the ongoing relevance of true prophetic ministry. Local churches are the most natural contest for the prophetic ministry, but when churches make no room for this ministry, those with prophetic stirrings will often be tempted to function outside their true sphere. Some gifted prophets who find that they are not received in local churches, have begun to direct their prophetic words to the secular nation, searching, for instance, for 'God's prophetic word for the UK'. Some will even hope for a latter-day John the Baptist to arise and address No. 10 Downing Street. My conviction is that the prophetic word to pagan Britain today is, 'Repent and believe the gospel!' This message is best proclaimed not by an individual prophet, but by a prophetic church living in obedience to God's word!

When Moses told downtrodden, captive Israel that God would soon release them, they were encouraged. Similarly, when today's prophet tells the church, 'You are not slaves but sons, not a laughing stock but a mighty army,' Christians rally to the battle cry. The vision lifts their sights. They see afresh the call to go into all the nations.

Prophetic gifting

The prophet brings direction and exhortation. Haggai told the people to go and get timber for God's house. His message was specific and thoroughly practical. A prophet proves that he is committed to the vision by being the first to respond to it. He leads the march and provides a foundation on which others build.

A prophet brings comfort, consolation and inner fortification. When Israel was overrun by the Babylonians,

Habakkuk knew that God was executing his judgement against his people. Yet the prophet also knew that the invaders would be brought to justice at God's appointed time. When Christians are going through pressure, they are comforted by prophecies which explain God's intentions.

A prophet brings solutions. The waters of Marah were bitter until Moses told the people to throw a tree into them (Ex 15:25). The church must expect God to reveal answers to many of its problems through prophetic gifts.

A prophet motivates action. When the prophets and teachers met to worship and fast at Antioch (Acts 13:1–3) they were not just having a good time of praise. They were concerned with God's prophetic purpose – how to reach the world with the gospel. We should be an active community that is encouraged and strengthened by the prophets (Acts 15:32).

God wants us to weigh prophecy. True prophecy never condemns or crushes us. It is instead something which edifies, exhorts or comforts us. It is always biblical, glorifies Jesus and has an 'upward' theme. It builds us up, stirs us up or cheers us up!

If we want to be a prophetic people we must respond to the prophetic word. Once the prophetic stream is moving, God will keep speaking into it. We must take care that we do not throw in defensiveness, hostility or cynicism and thus break the flow. When we hear from God, we need to act and not be taken up with the difficulties that may result. God told the Israelites to go into the Promised Land, but they were more concerned about the giants. Many churches are wandering in the wilderness today because they resisted the prophetic and focused on the problems.

There may be difficulties, but we must respond to the word. God wants to speak to his people and then through them to the world. We need to be captivated by what he says and swift at putting it into practice. Our church should be throbbing with prophetic life and motivated by prophetic vision.

Prophetic vision

'Without vision the people perish.' They also get side-tracked into preoccupation with present worries and relative trivialities. Many a congregation contains excellent people, but they are not sufficiently exposed to the prophetic ministry and so fail to be excited by God's ultimate purpose. Short-term problems dominate their thinking and prevent radical change. Even in the midst of spiritual renewal, such congregations fail to grasp what the renewing is for and where God is taking them. The prophet's voice needs to come like an axe to the root of our problems. The prophet has the incisive clarity of vision to cut through rubbish and search out motives and intentions. He forces us to ask uncomfortable questions that lead to uncomfortable answers. He causes the leaders of churches to re-examine their activities in the light of the principles that God has shown them. Often the diagnosis demands drastic surgery that elders would have shrunk from on their own.

The prophet is not simply a preacher, though he will preach. He is not simply an expositor of the Bible, though his great burden is to bring us back to the Bible and its authority.

Prophets bring people revelation and clarity concerning God's purpose for their time. Jeremiah, for instance, had to burst the balloon of false trust in outward religion, calling Judah to true dependence on God, not just on his temple (Jer 7:4). While they continued depending on their traditions as if they had all the time in the world, Jeremiah had to warn them that their time was rapidly running out.

The prophet must have room not only to speak at large conferences, but also to come into our churches. We must be prepared for him to expose our weaknesses so that we might change.

Clarity of vision keeps us from activity that is not centred on the ultimate goal. When the vision of the kingdom of God fills our horizon it will affect our whole lifestyle, our values and our decisions. As a young Christian I was taught no true vision for the church. Raised on dispensationalism, I was told that we were living in the Laodicean age and the Lord's return was our only hope. The whole emphasis of my evangelical life was 'personal'. I had a 'personal' saviour, practised 'personal' evangelism and pursued 'personal' devotions. No one told me that God had promised his Son the nations as his inheritance and the ends of the earth as his possession (Ps 2:8), or that the increase of his government would know no end (Is 9:7) and that the saints of the Most High would receive the kingdom and possess it for ever (Dan 7:18), and that these glorious promises somehow included me!

Though our church was keen on missionary work it was never taught, 'He will bring forth justice to the nations ... He will not be disheartened or crushed, until He has established justice in the earth; and the coastlands will wait expectantly for His law' (Is 42:1, 4, NASB). By contrast, missionary work consisted of isolated stabs at Satan's strongholds.

Now, however, we are beginning to understand the great implications of his magnificent prophetic statements for the church and for the nations of the world. People's lives have been changed by encountering and embracing prophetic vision. Within our ranks there are those who have turned down promotion for the sake of the kingdom and have been willing to jeopardise their career if to advance it meant being transferred to a place where there was no kingdom activity.

Some have tried to dismiss the prophetic gift by arguing that a prophet is simply a preacher or teacher, but the lists of gifts in Ephesians 4:11, 1 Corinthians 12:28 and Romans 12:6–7 are consistent in differentiating between them. Why does the Holy Spirit record them as different if they are simply the same gift, and what are we missing in the church without their ministry?

Listening to a prophet is not like listening to a teacher. The prophet will sometimes sound unbalanced. For a while he will sound as though he has only one message. His burden will not be to make sure that the balance is correct, but that the present issue is being resolved. It will be the local elders' responsibility to work out the detailed implications of the grand sweep of the prophetic vision. Often his insights will need the wisdom of apostolic ministry to bring the balance necessary to build safely for the future. Prophetic vision in tandem with apostolic wisdom is a powerful combination from the living God to build living churches. In our next chapter we will consider the role of the apostle today.

AND SOME APOSTLES

M y sister had just been converted and was trying to convert me. During our conversation she said, 'I'm not afraid of death any more; I know I'm going to heaven.' It was the most presumptuous thing I had ever heard. How could anyone know they were going to heaven? Later that evening I myself was born again and understood that salvation was all through the grace of God – his wonderful gift. I knew I had everlasting life.

Some sixteen years later I heard some of my friends discussing whether or not they were apostles. Again, I was quick to judge. What arrogance! Who did they think they were?

Now I have come to see that the call to salvation and the call to ministry both come by the grace of God. Paul received not only the grace of salvation but also the grace to be an apostle, though he was 'the very least of all saints' (Eph 3:8, NASB) and 'not fit to be called an apostle' (1 Cor 15:9, NASB).

Back to the Bible

My problem regarding conversion was solved by getting back to the Bible instead of walking in a maze of human logic based on previous experience. What does the natural mind know about salvation? Nothing at all. I had to submit to God's revelation in his word. Likewise with the question of apostleship. Can we dispense with apostles today? We may arrive at a variety of conclusions if we simply pool our own ideas. If we yield to the Bible, however, we shall find the true answer.

What is an apostle? The Greek word for apostle has its root in the verb 'to send', so apostle basically means 'a sent one'. Jesus repeatedly referred to himself as one, having been sent from the Father. Bishop Lightfoot tells us in his commentary on Galatians that the apostle is 'not only the messenger but the delegate of the person who sends him. He is entrusted with a mission and has powers conferred upon him' (J. B. Lightfoot, *St Paul's Epistle to the Galatians*, Macmillan & Co., 1981, p. 94).

Three classes

We can distinguish three classes of apostle in the New Testament. First of all there is Jesus, 'the Apostle and High Priest of our confession' (Heb 3:1, NASB). Next there are 'the twelve'. Some feel that this is the end of the story, and that Paul was raised up by God to replace Judas. It is argued that we never hear of the hastily appointed Matthias again; but actually we never hear of many of the twelve again, and the Bible nowhere states that Paul was one of the twelve. He clearly distinguishes himself from them in 1 Corinthians 15:5–8. The twelve were 'apostles of the Lamb' (Rev 21:14), called by Jesus during his earthly ministry. The replacement for Judas had to be one who had accompanied them from the beginning.

It could almost be argued that Paul is in a category of his own as 'one untimely born' (1 Cor 15:8, NASB). He was certainly given an extraordinary amount of revelation to contribute to the Scriptures. He was, nevertheless, commissioned by the ascended Christ, and must therefore be regarded as generally belonging to the category referred to in Ephesians 4:8–11, where we read that 'He ascended on high ... and He gave some as apostles'.

Special pleading might also be made for James, the brother of Jesus (Gal 1:19), who emerged as a leading apostle even though he seems to have been an unbeliever during Jesus' earthly ministry. In the council at Jerusalem he seems to have obtained an even more influential place than Paul or even Peter (Acts 15:13–21). Barnabas is also called an apostle (Acts 14:14), and his apostleship was recognised by the church at the same time as Paul's. Paul also speaks of Andronicus and Junias as being 'outstanding among the apostles, and they were in Christ before I was' (Rom 16:7).

Only twelve?

Many have argued that there were only twelve apostles, but as Bishop Lightfoot points out in his commentary on Galatians, 'Neither the canonical scriptures nor the early Christian writings afford sufficient ground for any such limitations of the apostolate.' Others have accepted that Paul, Barnabas and James were apostles, but still claim that the apostolic ministry is a thing of the past. Howard Snyder writes:

> Some have argued that apostles no longer exist today, but this conclusion runs counter to Biblical evidence ... Nothing in Paul's treatment of spiritual gifts suggests that he was describing a pattern for the early church only. Quite the opposite. For Paul, the church is a growing, grace-filled body, and apostles are a permanent part of that body's life. (Howard A. Snyder, *Community of the King*, InterVarsity Press, 1977)

Many who have reluctantly conceded that the gift of tongues might still be with us have continued to dismiss it by saying it is only the least of the gifts. The apostolic gift, if it is for today, certainly cannot be similarly shrugged off. After Jesus ascended, he gave apostles, prophets, evangelists and pastor/teachers to equip the saints until the church is brought to full maturity (Eph 4:12–13). We must not miss the vital word 'until'. Few would argue that the church has reached its full stature, and if any of these grace gifts are missing we will not reach God's intended goal.

We have epistles, who needs apostles?

It has been suggested that apostles are no longer needed today because we have the Bible. The New Testament letters of the original apostles are enough. Any Bible teacher can expound these great truths.

Some of our greatest teachers have indeed expounded the epistles with extraordinary life and power. However, the tragic fact is that instead of producing a mature church, held together by joints of supply with each part working properly (Eph 4:16), they have produced preaching centres with huge congregations that disintegrate when the gifted preacher is removed from the scene.

That does not mean we should despise great Bible teachers. Far from it! But what is our goal in building the church? Surely it is that in the end we have a mature expression of the body of Christ. The saints are not only to know sound doctrine, but are also to be equipped for works of service. They have to find their particular gifts and contributions to church life and should be encouraged to function in them. All the gifts of the ascended Christ are needed to reach this maturity.

The apostles of the early church did not fulfil only the role of writing the inspired New Testament. (Only a few of the apostles actually wrote our New Testament, helped by others such as Luke, who claimed no apostolic calling.) Just as in the Old Testament there were prophets who contributed nothing to Scripture, yet fulfilled a genuine prophetic ministry, so there were New Testament apostles who never gave us a line of Scripture, yet had a vital role to fulfil among the churches of their day.

Master builder

One of the distinctive features of the apostle is that he is a master builder and foundation layer (1 Cor 3:10). Paul did not regard his apostleship as a position in the church hierarchy. He did not see himself at the top of a corporate pyramid; he was not a chief executive in a complicated church superstructure.

Paul had a stewardship from God: he was to proclaim the unfathomable riches of Christ and bring people to an assured understanding of what it is to be in Christ and have Christ in them. This was the burden of apostolic doctrine. Paul did not wonder what he would preach from town to town; he had a body of doctrine to deliver. He knew when the saints had grasped it, and he knew when they had drifted from it. He could see the creeping death of legalism moving over one congregation and warned another against the subtle dangers of mystic Gnosticism. Modern churches still need the authoritative word that will set them free from legalism, super-spirituality and other dangers.

Many an Evangelical has thought liberalism to be the great enemy, not recognising other, perhaps more subtle, foes. Legalism, for instance, can look like commendable zeal; but Paul had no hesitation in calling it another gospel, not to be received even from an angel. How many in the average evangelical church are deeply assured that they have been delivered from sin, have died to the law, and are free from all condemnation? Apostolic doctrine handled with apostolic authority and insight is desperately needed.

Often we are blind to our own faults or shortcomings. Sometimes wrong emphases can enter in, hardly noticed by a local church focusing on itself. Spiritual coldness, doctrinal off-centredness, or incorrect practice can unobtrusively become part of a church's life.

One of God's great provisions to safeguard his church from going astray is a continuing apostolic ministry. The apostle, essentially a travelling man, is able to bring objectivity to his appraisal of a local church's condition. For instance, although the church in Thessalonica was in many ways exemplary, Paul wrote to the believers there that he longed to see them so he could supply what was lacking in their faith (1 Thess 3:10).

Others, such as the saints in Corinth, Galatia and Colossae, had much for which to thank God in Paul's care of their churches.

Feeling the need

To illustrate further, if a local church, for instance, has not only received an attitude of legalism but has actually built some of its church structure around it, who has the authority to bring correction? The elders often feel trapped within the framework and long for an outside voice to proclaim the way forward authoritatively. Indeed, it is very often the elders who most feel the need for the apostolic ministry. At a recent ministers' conference I addressed, it was acknowledged that, even if they could not yet see all the scriptural basis for apostolic ministry, the ministers personally felt the need for such a figure to arise to help them in their leadership of the congregation.

Traditional churches are feeling the pressures of new life. Charismatic gifts are emerging; a desire for freer worship is being expressed. How are the leaders to proceed? Many are facing such issues and do not know which way to turn. Conferences for like-minded pastors will not provide the full answer, nor will charismatic organisations. God's way is to give apostles and prophets. He has simply appointed servants with different gifts to do different jobs.

Paul's authority was not derived from a special title or office. It was the fruit of two things: first, the grace of God in calling and equipping him with a particular gift as an apostle, and secondly, the working relationship he had with any particular church or individual. For example, Paul's fatherly relationship towards the churches in Corinth, Galatia and Thessalonica is plain to see. He wrote to the Corinthians, '... in Christ Jesus I became your father through the gospel' (1 Cor 4:15). He rejoiced in their lives and their love, and wept over their failures and shortcomings. As their father he lovingly and forthrightly claimed spiritual authority among them.

When writing to the church at Rome, however, Paul's style was different. He felt free to communicate, but he did not adopt the same approach he had used with other churches. He had not yet seen the Roman church face to face; they were not his 'children in the Lord'.

Eldership appointment

Paul's fatherly care for the church was also demonstrated in his concern that they have local leaders. The appointment of elders was an important aspect of his church building programme. The Holy Spirit selected elders, but they received public recognition through the laying on of hands by the apostles or their delegates.

Modern churches have often resorted to electing their leaders, but those elected into office can similarly be voted out of office, so the temptation to be a man-pleaser is considerable. Appointed by the congregation, such leaders are accountable to the congregation. When there is no anointing, democracy is probably the safest form of church government. But when God begins to give anointed leadership, democracy must make room for him to have his way.

In the New Testament the whole matter was far more charismatic, in the word's truest sense. The Spirit-led appointment of elders was an important part of the apostles' foundation-laying ministry. Without the Holy Spirit's guidance, we resort to man-made structures with varying degrees of success, even leading to manifest disaster. In recent days some have even found it difficult to elect new leaders because differences of opinion in the congregation make the required majority hard to find. Where there is no acknowledgement of charismatic gifts of leadership we are bound to hit problems.

The wise master builder will not select elders of his own choice in an arbitrary way. He will observe the way in which men have earned the respect and love of the people and are displaying the fact that God himself has appointed them. The laying on of hands then becomes an outward acknowledgement of what God has done by his Spirit. It is also a time of further impartation of spiritual grace for eldership.

Regions beyond

Another major aspect of the work of an apostle is breaking new ground with the gospel. Paul was always looking for virgin territory where new churches could be built. As he set sail, he inspired existing churches with his outreaching vision.

Paul planned to see the church at Rome on his way to Spain and be helped on his way by them (Rom 15:24); so the Roman church was drawn into the apostle's missionary thrust into Spain. Members of Paul's team kept the churches informed of his movements, and kept him informed of the churches' progress. Young Timothys were caught up in the world vision and were trained in the apostolic team. They learned in living situations.

So, just as local pastors reproduce after their kind at home, apostles reproduce after their kind while on their apostolic journeys. Soon Timothy or Titus could be sent with Paul's full blessing to do the job he himself would have done. Thus the work was multiplied.

As a result of their travels the apostles not only opened up new areas but brought a sense of unity to the work of God at large. Because of this unity, Paul was able, through his contacts, to bring not only spiritual help but also material help to churches in need. The poor in Jerusalem, for example, were helped by the churches Paul visited elsewhere. It is clear from the New Testament that God never intended local churches to be isolated. Through their relationships, with the unifying work of an apostle, they are caught up in an international fellowship and in the worldwide spreading of the gospel. People in local churches who have no larger vision are often tempted to become inward-looking and negative; but where there is global vision and the stimulus of news from other growing churches, there is a strong desire for expansion.

What do you want to build?

Can we do without apostles? The answer very much depends on what we are aiming to build. If we want simply to preserve the status quo, certainly we can cope without them. If we want a nice, cosy, charismatic house group or a safe institutional church enjoying a little renewal now and then, we can find some of our hopes fulfilled. But if we want to see the church come to the fullness of the stature of Christ, to a mature man, it is essential for all the gifted people mentioned in Ephesians 4 to have their full place in our church life.

How do apostles emerge? Like evangelists and prophets, they are brought out by the sovereign choice and anointing of God. Thus there is no apostolic succession, nor is there any one training ground that produces all these leaders. Paul emerged from a background different from that of the other apostles, but needed the assurance that those he knew to be apostles before him recognised his calling and would extend the right hand of fellowship to him, which, in fact, they were happy to do (Gal 2:9).

If the apostle is only to work on virgin soil where Christ has not been named, is there any room in the West for apostles today? Christ is certainly named throughout the Western nations, but we all know in what way many of the 90% outside our churches use that name.

Church planting

The fact remains that if we are to see the tide turn in the nations, we need to plant a great number of new churches – churches that are healthy, powerful communities built firmly on God's word and relevant to modern society. Such new churches *are* being planted today, motivated and overseen by apostolic ministry. In addition, churches that have been in existence for many years often seek the aid of this ministry to help them through barriers they have found impossible to penetrate on their own.

Several Old Testament books describe the work of restoration that took place after the Babylonian captivity. As Paul said, 'These things happened to them as an example, and they were written for our instruction, upon whom the ends of the ages have come' (1 Cor 10:11, NASB). We can identify wholly with Ezra and Nehemiah in the rebuilding programme and also derive great encouragement from Haggai and Zechariah as we rebuild the ruins of church life. Like Ezra, we need to recover fully the place of the Scriptures; and like Nehemiah, we find that much rubbish needs to be removed. Great tenacity is called for to see the recovery work completed.

Not imposed authority

One part of the contemporary apostle's role is to bring the measuring line to church life to see if it matches up with biblical standards. That is not to say he will arrive uninvited at any local church to declare his judgements. If the mighty apostle Paul was not automatically recognised by all as an apostle, and if his presence was regarded by some as unimpressive and contemptible, we can be sure that far lesser apostles would find it very difficult to impose their authority, or, indeed, to be recognised at all!

The modern apostle will be regarded by some as simply a brother or a preacher, while to others he functions as an apostle. That presents no problem; it is not unlike the attitude Christians might have towards local pastor/teachers from other churches in their area. The uninvited apostle cannot impose his authority in other churches; nor should it be his desire to do so. He will, however, happily respond to requests from church elders who reach out for his help.

The modern apostle makes no claims to infallibility, and surely our understanding is that only God's word is infallible, not the actions of even New Testament apostles. Hence we see Paul having to correct Peter for his wrongful action in connection with the circumcision advocates (Gal 1:11–14). Surely no modern apostle would seek to put himself above the apostle Peter. We can rejoice that we now have the completed Scriptures, not to *replace* spiritual gifts or the Ephesians 4 ministries, but as a means by which we may *test* them to be assured that they are of God.

Apostolic teams

Like Paul, the modern apostle will find he cannot work alone. As the work multiplies he will draw colleagues to his side. We have coined the phrase 'apostolic team', but we must be careful not to suggest something official by that title. There is no such thing as 'team status'. Paul sometimes moved with some men, sometimes with others. They did not thereby claim a peculiar position as 'team member'. The arrangement was purely functional and very fluid.

In sending Timothy, Paul was confident that he would remind them of 'my ways which are in Christ, just as I teach everywhere in every church' (1 Cor 4:17, NASB). The men who travelled with Paul, and who were sent to and from him, multiplied the ministry. Their relationship with Paul provided a setting in which they no doubt developed their own 'ways in Christ'; they would keep a strong dependence on Paul, but would also develop their own special contribution.

Some men travelling with an apostle will be like Barnabas – former local leaders who have proved their worth at a flourishing home church that is now sufficiently secure to release them. Others will be young men like Timothy, who not only commend themselves to the apostle, but also have excellent relationships with local elders, who sense the hand of God upon them and release them gladly to the larger work.

Care for the churches

So we have a company of men who know that their prime calling is no longer to one particular local work – though their roots are there – but to the church at large. Whereas once they had the care of a local flock, they begin to develop a care for the churches – plural (2 Cor 11:28).

Within the so-called 'team' there will be embryonic apostles like Timothy; there will also be those with other gifts – prophets or evangelists, for instance – whose roles will differ, but who find a 'team' relationship truly helpful in keeping them from being isolated and vulnerable.

It is important to see that prophets, evangelists and pastor/teachers have different ministries and therefore will not try to bring to a local church what in the end only an apostle can bring. There is a danger, when a man moves into a different area of anointing, that he will be ineffective, resulting in frustration and insecurity. For instance, when trying to represent the apostle, the pastor who is not truly apostolic may tend to hold back where he should be decisive. Failing to recognise fundamental problems in a church he may continue to encourage and build up the people when really some 'tearing down' must take place first. His gifts of teaching and caring are best used when a good foundation is already laid in terms of doctrine, practice and eldership. Like a dentist who knows there is more decay in a tooth which must be removed before a filling can be added, the apostle will insist on basic changes in doctrine, style, structure or leadership personnel before simply building up the people with encouraging ministry.

Alternatively a pastor may compensate for lack of apostolic anointing by undue legalism and 'going by the book' which promotes a system instead of life. The prophet will excite activity, but will tend to breed insecurity when he is not joined to an apostle. The evangelist will gather many people, but will not build them together. As a team bound with an apostle in love and mutual respect, they become a mighty force in the kingdom of God.

Paul's travels took him across national borders from country to country. Often he was separated for long periods of time from churches he had fathered. By modern means of communication and travel, the twentieth-century apostle and his colleagues can be in much closer contact with the churches they serve. By telephone we can reach around the world by dialling a few numbers; by motorways we can travel miles for an evening's meeting; by jet plane we can circle the globe in a few hours; by printed books and audio and video cassettes we can speak when we are not even present.

There are no international barriers to apostolic ministry, and, in fact, at one time the company travelling with Paul comprised men from several nations (Acts 20:4). Apostolic ministry transcends nationalism and does not attempt to superimpose one nation's culture on another. Some travelling ministers will count it their joy to stimulate the development of emerging apostles and prophets in other nations, and then to step back to let them fulfil their calling, as Barnabas did with Paul. God will thus raise up Antioch churches all over the world – churches of far-reaching vision that release fresh apostolic and prophetic ministry.

PLANTING NEW CHURCHES

I have seen it happen many times now – sometimes a handful of Christians gathering in a home; sometimes a small group dwarfed by the school hall they have hired. Everything seems vulnerable and in miniature. Planting a new church is not easy but, if we handle it well, it is the most effective way of evangelising a new area.

Who should start a new church? The New Testament does not seem to give one simple answer. Philip the evangelist penetrated Samaria, saw many converts and gathered a community. The apostle Paul operated similarly in many towns. But not only apostles and evangelists founded new churches. It seems that scattered, persecuted believers went everywhere preaching the gospel. Even the influential Antioch church was started by unnamed believers, helped later by the arrival of Barnabas sent from the apostolic base in Jerusalem.

Jesus said that the field is the world and the seed is the sons of the kingdom (Mt 13:37–38). That seed can be sown with great evangelistic effect. In other words, a number of believers moving into a new area can start a church drawing help from the visits of travelling foundation-laying ministries. People can be released from their existing church and town to get involved in this great project. Who should go? I can imagine some pastors very happily selecting some of their members whom they would like to send to another town and preferably as far away as possible!

The reality is that we are not actually looking for those who are surplus to requirements, or people whose call we are happy to confirm for the wrong reasons.

Nor should those who are merely frustrated with their present home base see this as guidance to move elsewhere. The best people to go are those who would be sadly missed and who are probably very fulfilled in the work they are already doing – though there may be those whom God has started unsettling as part of the process leading up to the uprooting that is about to take place.

Those who go must demonstrate several genuine spiritual strengths if they are going to see success. First, they must be visionaries, people whose faith can sustain them during the difficult early days. Visionaries tend to look forward, not backward. Abraham was happy to live in a tent, not because he preferred tent dwelling to the comforts of Ur of the Chaldees, but because he had seen something else. He was not gripped by tent life but by his vision of the city that God had impressed upon him.

Similarly, those who endure the pains and problems of starting a new church must be strongly motivated by a God-given vision of the congregation that will grow around them. They must not be preoccupied with comparisons with what they enjoyed before. There may be many areas of weakness. The meeting place, the stewarding, the heating, the parking space, the children's work, the ability of musicians – all may conspire to make the new congregation feel vulnerable. The atmosphere of uncertainty can make people feel very insecure. If you are not strongly motivated by a forward-looking vision that motivates faith and makes you happily endure early difficulties, you may want to give up and go back. It only needs a couple of mid-winter Sundays when the school caretaker forgets to switch on the heating to cool your zeal.

Those involved need to be flexible and open to change. Often meeting places have to be abandoned. One of the churches we planted had at least six different meeting places before it found a permanent home. Disappointments and delay can dog your steps, so endurance and steadfastness must characterise the initiating group. Young people and children can find that they are no longer part of a flourishing youth group and they have virtually no contemporaries in their new setting. Being the only teenager in a new church provides quite a challenge!

Spiritual opposition can also be expected. This may even take the form of hostility from other churches that do not appreciate your arrival. Strength of purpose and inward courage must win the day at such times. These strengths need also to be balanced by teachability and a clear willingness to be led. Humility towards the new church's leadership and also towards other local Christians is required. Strong-minded people with their own personal agendas are no asset in a new church planting, so great strengths must be tempered by grace and meekness. Warmth and hospitality should also be in great supply or growth will never take place. Simply planting a group of Christians from one town to another is no guarantee of evangelistic success. Christian ghettos can form very easily. Real growth requires an outgoing group of people. With this in mind we have found it almost essential to make sure that every new church planting has an evangelist in its leadership team. A full-time pastor teamed with a full-time evangelist proves a healthy combination, especially when also drawing on a short-term evangelistic group in support. (We often supply year teams or brief visit 'Frontier Teams'.)

Where do we plant?

Paul seemed to aim at strategic cities but he also responded to specific interventions from the Holy Spirit who, for instance, forbade him to go to Asia and led him very specifically to Macedonia.

When Paul started his outreach he travelled initially to Cyprus. Why? It seems that his own Antioch base was started by believers from Cyprus, so perhaps he was simply following natural links. We should not despise such developments. Eight years ago I asked a friend, Don Smith, who led the Kings Church at Hastings, how many of his people worked in nearby Eastbourne. He discovered that about two dozen of his congregation made the daily trip. I asked him to consider moving there and inviting the two dozen to move with him. He immediately felt that this was the Holy Spirit's guidance. Lex Loizides, a young evangelist converted in my home church in Brighton, joined him. There is now a flourishing new church in Eastbourne with about 200 in attendance and having recently bought a large warehouse for their meeting place. I remember attending their second Sunday when under thirty people sat in a circle of chairs in a large school hall, looking very vulnerable indeed! I also remember the joyful spirit of faith that was among them and I praise God for the encouraging growth that he has given them.

On another occasion we became aware that a growing number of people were being moved from the South East of England by their secular employment since there was something of an economic crisis at that time. I invited a colleague to do some research for me and see if any one town featured in these moves. Manchester topped the list. My friend, Colin Baron, began to realise that he was not only handling some research, but was being stirred by God to initiate the developments that were to follow.

Graham Webb, an evangelist from the church we had planted in Horsham, felt motivated to join him, so in 1993 the two families moved. In March 1996 I spoke at the freshly planted Burnage Family Church in Manchester. There were now 200 present and on the previous Sunday they had already released fifty people to North Manchester for their own first church plant led by Rob Coleman, who originated from the church we started in Crawley. They aim to start twenty churches in the Greater Manchester area and now have two congregations built on their prophetic vision.

Another pastor friend of mine felt increasingly stirred about the city of Cambridge. Again we did some research and found how many from within New Frontiers Churches across the UK were studying at university there. David Coak began to meet with a small nucleus. He found a house and moved. Some of his friends from his former church base in Sussex accompanied him and a group started. A young evangelist, Mark Anstead, from the church we had planted in Canterbury some five years earlier, moved to accompany him. Now between 150 and 200 gather each week at a healthy and growing church in Cambridge.

Timing is a key issue in the matter of church planting. The apostle Paul seemed to be continually looking to see if God had 'opened a door' for him. He was aware of a spiritual dimension which demonstrated God's commitment. For instance, although he experienced persecution in Corinth he also heard God tell him that he had many people in that city.

Some church plantings with which I have been associated have originated in a strong sense of guidance on the part of the leader. Others have come about by the fact that a group already travelled in from another town to attend a particular church because of the absence of a church in their own area. The church led by Ray Lowe in Biggin Hill, Kent, for instance, has planted several churches on this basis. Because they themselves have been a vibrant and attractive community they have found companies of people travelling in to be with them for a season. They have then been trained, and leadership has emerged from their ranks, whereupon they have themselves been planted back out to form new churches in surrounding towns.

Sometimes new churches of this sort can originate in the 'womb' of the existing 'mother' church. They can begin to form an identity while still within the protection of the parent body. The leadership can start to gather those who will form the embryo church, though for a season they know the safety of being in the larger group. When the time comes for being planted out, relationships can already have been developed and a sense of identity already been formed. This kind of planting has usually proved extremely effective. Often evangelism begins to take place more quickly since the people involved already live in the neighbourhood of the new church and can now invite their neighbours to a meeting place that is at hand instead of at a distance. Churches formed in this way continue to enjoy the blessing of ongoing care and oversight from travelling apostolic and prophetic ministry and so a group of churches begins to form.

It is vital that those being planted out regard themselves as 'on a mission' and have a real evangelistic motivation. Where our plantings have lacked that motivation, but have simply wanted a nice, cosy congregation nearer home, no serious impact has been made on Satan's territory. This is where the persistent involvement of those in travelling ministry is crucial.

House churches

I personally have been involved in this kind of church planting since the early 1970s. Over the years I have helped to form a number of new churches, mostly across the county of Sussex. They took the form of 'house churches' in those early days and actually had no relationship with one another but simply enjoyed my regular visits. Now all of those churches have outgrown their 'house church' beginnings and meet in large hired halls or buildings they have bought.

Gradually, as the number of churches grew, I also became involved with existing churches that heard of this development. A number of churches in South London, for instance, invited me to help them. Some pastors who were already good friends had embraced the charismatic movement in their ranks but had difficulties in adjusting their churches into this new phase. I was asked, on the basis of my experience, to help the people in these churches to understand and welcome the new developments. So I now found myself involved with some totally new churches and some existing churches that were seeking help.

When New Frontiers International was made up of seventy churches, a friend asked me how many we had started and how many we had 'adopted'. I literally had no idea, so for the first time I counted and found that exactly thirty-five were new churches and thirty-five had their own previous history but had subsequently invited my involvement. (That pattern has roughly continued, as the current number of churches in NFI has grown to 170, of which 128 are in the UK.)

Initially, I simply became personally involved with churches that had no common identity, but there came a day when God impressed upon me the need to bring these churches into an active interrelationship. I was praying with a number of pastors when one received a vision. He saw a herd of elephants charging through undergrowth, trampling it down and creating a new road. The opening words of his prophecy were, 'There are no well-worn paths ahead of you.' He went on to say that we would accomplish more together than we ever could alone.

As a result of this prophecy and other current leading, I gathered all the pastors of the churches I was serving at that time and told them that I felt God was calling us to have some public common identity. I felt that the title 'New Frontiers' was being impressed upon me, representing the fact that God was calling us to penetrate new territory both geographically and in our spiritual experience. I explained to the brothers a change of philosophy in my thinking and offered them freedom to withdraw from associating with me if this brought them any disquiet. To my delight no one wanted to withdraw and so the name 'New Frontiers International' was born, and although each church that I work with selects its own name it is also happy to be known as being in association or partnership with the New Frontiers International team. This means that we are working together to a common vision. God has impressed upon me the goals of restoring the church, making disciples, training leaders, planting churches and reaching the nations. All those with whom we work, either new or existing churches, embrace these common goals and join us on our mission.

It is impossible to 'join us' by simply changing your church's name or approaching 'headquarters'. Though we have vision and values, there is no rule book. Nor is it possible to become identified with us without a genuine friendship and relationship. In fact the New Frontiers International title is simply a label used to identify those churches who are in living relationship with me and a team of men with whom I work.

Unity and diversity

Although all the churches planted or embraced into this fellowship own common values, we encourage a great deal of diversity in local church life. For instance, there has never been any instruction from me concerning the frequency or style of the breaking of bread. Attitudes towards the inclusion of children in Sunday meetings and house groups would vary enormously. Some include children in their meetings from beginning to end, others for part of the service, others again would not expect the children to join them at all for their weekly public meetings. The style of house groups differs considerably, though I feel it would be of very high value to see small groups of one kind or another in local church life since I believe that without small group life individuals will never grow to spiritual maturity.

Some churches have developed ministry to the poor and homeless. Others have developed diverse specialist ministries. Some have deacons, others do not. The establishing of ministers' salaries is totally a matter for the local church and not something that I have ever become involved with. Different churches use different styles of evangelistic endeavour, often reflecting the gifting and anointing in their ranks. I would never try to enforce a style of evangelism, though I would strongly urge that evangelism should take place and I am currently recommending churches to consider the cell church system and the Alpha course as they are powerfully effective.

So what is it that holds us together? A common vision, which is to restore the church, make disciples, train leaders, plant churches and reach the nations. We build together as friends in a strong personal relationship, honouring the spiritual gifts that are scattered among us. We also take seriously God's sovereign direction in our lives which gives us the inner peace that God himself has drawn us together.

Some might fear that these kinds of relationship represent what Paul opposed in 1 Corinthians 3:4 when he rejected the 'I am of Paul' slogan. The fact remains that in the same epistle Paul admonished them as his beloved children and said that although they had countless tutors they did not have many fathers. In Christ Jesus he had become their father through the gospel and they were to imitate him (1 Cor 3:4; 4:14). Undoubtedly he hated the divisions in the body demonstrated by the Corinthians, but he did not deny his personal relationship with them. He rebuked élitism and party spirit, but acknowledged his fathering role.

Paul also added that he was sending Timothy as his beloved and faithful child to remind them of his ways in Christ as he taught them in every church. In 2 Corinthians 8:1 he spoke of the churches in Macedonia that first gave themselves to the Lord and also 'to us'. In 1 Corinthians 9:1 he argues that they were his 'work in the Lord'.

'All the churches'

One of Paul's favourite phrases is 'all the churches'. For example, in 1 Corinthians 7:17 he speaks of his teaching on a certain theme and concludes: 'Thus I direct in all the churches' (NASB). The question arises – what did Paul mean by his phrase 'all the churches'? Did he mean every church that existed at that time in the known world? It would be difficult to reach that conclusion if we consider Paul's words in Galatians 1:22, where he says that he was unknown to the churches of Judea which were in Christ Jesus. Therefore it is hard for us to argue that his reference to 'all the churches' included churches where he was personally unknown. Given this, Paul's phrase 'all the churches' presumably meant all the churches in which he was particularly involved. He had a care of 'all the churches', which was perhaps similar to a pastor who has the care of all the people in his congregation, though he wanted no one to boast in men. 'For all things belong to you, whether Paul or Apollos, or Cephas ... and you belong to Christ and Christ belongs to God' (1 Cor 3:21–23, NASB).

Paul had a zeal for the unity of the whole church and argued in Ephesians 2:14 that God had made both groups one, breaking down the dividing wall and making one new man. Yet the same apostle taught in Galatians 2:7 that God had sent him to the Gentiles and Peter to the Jews. In other words his theology argued for the unity of the church, yet his pragmatic experience was that some men had one sphere and some another. He was unafraid to tell the Corinthians, 'If to others I am not an apostle, at least I am to you' (1 Cor 9:2, NASB).

Paul clearly had a unique relationship with a number of churches, several of which he had brought to birth, some of which he had never seen face to face. Epaphras, for instance, had been involved with the birth of the church at Colosse and also travelled with the apostle Paul. In his letter to the Colossians Paul sent Epaphras' greetings, reminding them that he was one of them, though currently with Paul. Through his relationship with Epaphras Paul had a strong link with Colosse. They came within his sphere of operation.

It is evident that Paul cared for these churches, prayed for them, served them and saw them as his base of operation from which he also reached to regions beyond them. His world mission was rooted in their love and support. It was his hope that as their faith grew he would have an even more enlarged sphere: 'Your growing faith will mean the expansion of our sphere of action' (2 Cor 10:15, J. B. PHILLIPS). He wanted to preach where Christ was not yet named so as not to build on another man's foundation (Rom 15:20).

As Paul travelled, he lifted the sights of local churches and gathered them into his world vision, so when writing to the church in Rome he mentioned that he not only wanted to visit them, but he also wanted them to help him on his way to Spain (Rom 15:24). Our own goal within New Frontiers International is not only to help plant local churches within the UK, but to help them get caught up in a programme of worldwide mission. In fact at one time we tended to be concentrated in the South East of England near to my own Sussex base and essentially around the London area, but God spoke to me in a vision showing me the South East of England with a bow superimposed over it. The string was then pulled back across the heart of England and into the North, an arrow placed pointing outwards from the South East. I felt God was communicating to me that we should endeavour to plant churches in the Midlands and North of England, not only with a view to evangelising within the UK, but also that, as a bow gains strength to shoot its arrow by pulling the arrow back, so we also would gain strength in terms of resources across the UK, thus energising our outreach to the ends of the earth.

It is very thrilling to know that people who have come into our ranks from across the UK have already found their way into other nations such as India, South Africa, Cyprus and Mexico through their fellowship with us in our mission. Ultimately our goal is not only to plant churches within the UK but across the world, with ongoing apostolic, prophetic and evangelistic ministry to help the local pastors and teachers and the flocks that gather around them. (We are also working with nationals in Denmark, Holland, Switzerland, Ghana, Sierra Leone, the UAE and the USA.)

We are together on a mission. Our individual delight in Jesus is being expressed by a spirit of adventure. Church planting and world evangelisation are gradually becoming a passion for many. Working together with a group of churches has made possible many strategies that would be beyond the scope of one local church. Sadly several long-standing missionary societies that have served God's purpose magnificently over many decades have felt that they cannot embrace charismatic gifts in their ranks, so those who have come to enjoy the benefits of these mighty tools must find new ways forward to fulfil the Great Commission. The recent outpouring of the Holy Spirit is helping us on our way, and the promise that every nation must be reached before the end comes is urging us forward. But more of this in our final chapter.

INTO ALL THE WORLD

All too often new Christians understand their conversion experience purely in terms of having their personal needs met. In a sense this need not be despised, since Jesus frequently gathered new converts on that basis. He offered them peace, forgiveness and living water to meet their raging thirst. He gathered the weary to his loving embrace.

The problem arises when powerful outpourings of the Holy Spirit are valued and interpreted with the same emphasis, namely with the goal of simply providing me with more emotional release and meeting even more of my personal needs. When the church turns all its blessings inwards it misses the point, fails to fulfil the Great Commission and eventually grows stagnant.

When God originally blessed Abraham it was not for his sake alone but that through him all the families of the earth would be blessed (Gen 12:1–3). He knew he was to 'be heir of the world' (Rom 4:13). God's blessing on him had world ramifications.

Abraham's children

We, who are now Abraham's children, need to adopt Abraham's stance. We are here to bless the nations! The Old Testament is full of promises that God would one day be worshipped by people from every nation. As the psalmist said, 'All the ends of the earth will remember and turn to the Lord, and all the families of the nations will bow down before him, for dominion belongs to the Lord and he rules over the nations' (Ps 22:27–28).

Isaiah believed that the truth which God had revealed to his tiny nation would reach all the people groups of the world and that they would ultimately bow the knee to Israel's Holy One. So the promise to Abraham is reflected in Isaiah 2: 'In the last days the mountain of the Lord's temple will be established as the chief among the mountains ... and all nations will stream to it' (Is 2:2). Joel promised that in the last days God would pour out his Spirit on all flesh and Isaiah promised that in these same last days all the nations would abandon their false gods in order to stream to Israel's God. Mission work is not a call to Westernise other cultures or bring them a British lifestyle or the American way. As Jesus said to the woman of Samaria, 'We worship that which we know, for salvation is from the Jews' (Jn 4:22, NASB). Soon after his statement the Samaritans streamed to him, the Jewish Messiah (Jn 4:30, NASB). Fulfilment of the ancient promise was beginning. The God of the Jews was to become the God of the nations.

These promises formed the foundation of New Testament missionary vision. Paul in Galatians reminded his readers that 'the Scripture, foreseeing that God would justify the Gentiles by faith, preached the gospel beforehand to Abraham, saying, "All the nations shall be blessed in you"' (Gal 3:8, NASB). Salvation was promised through Abraham and his seed. Paul, with New Testament revelation, interpreted that promise for us in Galatians when he showed us that the seed was Christ and went on to show us that if we are Christ's we are Abraham's offspring and heirs of the promise (Gal 3:7, 29). In reading such passages we must not allow anyone to give us an interpretation of the Old Testament that is contrary to the writings of the New Testament. The New Testament writers themselves are the only infallible interpreters.

As J. I. Packer says,

> Jesus was the appointed and anointed Christ, the Son of God both officially and personally, the maker and master

of all things, the Lord of all life, the determiner of all destinies, and the Saviour of all his servants. From him and his Messianic ministry his church would derive its identity; to him in his Messianic glory it would give its loyalty. It would be his church in every sense.

Nor would the founding of it be in any sense a breakaway from the past. On the contrary, Christ's church was to be, and now is, nothing more nor less than the Old Testament covenant community itself, in a new and fulfilled form that God had planned for it from the start. It is Israel internationalised and globally extended in, through, and under the unifying dominion of Jesus the divine Saviour who is its King (J. I. Packer, *A Passion for Faithfulness*, Crossway Books, 1995)

All the glorious promises of international impact for the people of God are wrapped up in the coming of the Christ, his suffering and death, resurrection and ascension to glory. The pentecostal outpouring of the Spirit heralded the New Covenant which Jeremiah promised (Jer 31:33–34). Now the Old Covenant is superseded, the new is written in our heart as Jeremiah promised and as Paul explained (2 Cor 3:3).

Fulfilled today!

When Jesus took the scroll in the synagogue at Nazareth (Lk 4:16–21) and read from the book of Isaiah (Is 61:1–2) he concluded by announcing, '*Today* this scripture is fulfilled in your hearing.' He went everywhere announcing the arrival of the promised kingdom. In him, the Servant of the Lord, all the promises were encapsulated. He was the light to the nations (Is 42:6). God identified him at his baptism in no uncertain way. The Promised One had come! 'This is my beloved Son.' He was the chosen one in whom God's soul delighted. He would bring justice to the nations (Is 42:1).

His disciples were to follow in his steps. Identifying themselves also as the fulfilment of Isaiah's 'Servant' prophecies (Acts 13:4,7; Is 49:6), they were now the world's light, teaching men in every nation to observe all things that Jesus commanded (Mt 28:18). Isaiah's prophetic promises are breaking out all over the world. Millions of Chinese, Koreans, South Americans, Africans and indeed people from every continent are finding Israel's God. They are abandoning their false gods in order to embrace the one that Isaiah saw 'high and lifted up, whose robe filled the Temple'. The suffering, yet triumphant Servant of the Lord graphically described in Isaiah 53 is sharing his spoils with the world. Amazing breakthroughs are taking place. The promised kingdom is advancing forcefully.

As John Bright says,

> Christ came, indeed, to announce the decisive redeeming act of God, and to perform it. But he did not come to inform Judaism of a new and unknown God. The New Testament then does not present us with a new religion which we may study for itself alone ... the Bible is one book. Had we to give that book a title we might with justice call it 'The Book of the Coming Kingdom of God'. That is indeed its central theme everywhere. In the New Testament, however, there is a difference; the Kingdom of God has become also the Kingdom of Christ and that Kingdom is actually at hand. (John Bright, *The Kingdom of God*, Abingdon Press, Nashville)

The early Christians went everywhere preaching this wonderful kingdom. They were a pilgrim people on the move, beseeching people to be reconciled to God.

As John Stott says,

> When the Spirit came in power, the long promised reign of God, which Jesus had himself inaugurated and proclaimed,

would begin to spread. It would be spiritual in its character (transforming the lives and values of its citizens), international in its membership (including Gentiles as well as Jews) and gradual in its expansion (beginning at once in Jerusalem, and then growing until it reaches the end of both time and earthly space) ... the Christian mission would radiate out from that centre in accordance with the ancient prophecy that 'the law will go out from Zion, the word of the Lord from Jerusalem' (Is 2:3). (John R. W. Stott, *The Message of Acts*, from The Bible Speaks Today series, IVP)

Sense of destiny

It is of colossal importance that the church rediscover her sense of destiny in the earth. It is no small thing to be the world's only light, to be the fulfilment of centuries of ancient prophetic promises, to be heralding the Day of the Lord, to hold the message of history in your hands and to be the world's one and only answer. It is our indescribable privilege to be caught up by the Holy Spirit in the greatest movement in history – the proclaiming of Christ to every tribe, tongue, people and nation.

As John Piper says,

It is men of faith who are the sons of Abraham ... 'If you are Christ's then you are Abraham's offspring, heirs according to the Promise' (Gal 3:7, 29). This is how Paul saw Abraham's blessing coming to the nations. It came through Christ who was the seed of Abraham. By faith people are united to Christ and inherit the blessing of Abraham. 'Christ redeemed us from the curse of the law ... and in Christ Jesus the blessing of Abraham might come upon the Gentiles' (Gal 3:13–14). So the promise of Genesis 12:3 comes true as the missionaries of the Christian church extend the message of the gospel to all the families of the earth.

When Paul read that Abraham would be made 'the father of many nations' he heard the Great Commission. These nations would only come into their sonship and enjoy the blessing of Abraham if missionaries reached them with the gospel of salvation by faith in Jesus Christ. It is not surprising then to find Paul supporting his own missionary calling with other Old Testament promises that predicted the reaching of the nations with God's light and salvation. (John Piper, *Let the Nations be Glad*, IVP)

World evangelisation is the greatest task that a Christian, a church, or a group of churches can embrace. It is the goal of history. It is what gives history meaning and purpose. Those being saved and added to local churches need to be exposed to a magnificent vision which is enough to captivate their imagination and arrest their energies. The local church should be so aware of its calling, so committed to God's ultimate purpose, that individual converts are set free from the futile way of life that they inherited from their forefathers so that they can give themselves unreservedly to God and his cause.

As Paul Billheimer says,

The final and ultimate outcome and goal of events from eternity to eternity, the finished product of all the ages, is the spotless Bride of Christ, united with Him in wedded bliss at the marriage supper of the Lamb and seated with her Heavenly Bridegroom upon the throne of the universe – ruling and reigning with him over an ever increasing and expanding kingdom. He entered the stream of human history for this one purpose, to claim his beloved. (Rev 19:6, 9; 21:7, 9, 10).

Thus the Church and only the Church is the key to and explanation of history. The Church, blood washed and spotless is the centre, the reason, and the goal of all of God's vast creative handiwork. Therefore, history is only the handmaiden of the Church, and the nations of the world are but puppets manipulated by God for the purposes of His Church (Acts 17:26). Creation has no other aim. History has no other goal. From before the foundation of the world until the dawn of eternal ages God has been working towards one grand event, one supreme end – the glorious wedding of His Son, the marriage supper of the Lamb. (Paul Billheimer, *Destined for the Throne*, CLC)

We, like Abraham, need to turn our backs on our former lifestyle and look for the city of God. We need to feel our hearts are set on pilgrimage and our faces looking towards all that God has for his glorious church in these end times.

There will undoubtedly be great hostility, and darkness may yet cover the earth and gross darkness the people, but God's light is arising on his church. We feel fresh outpourings of the Holy Spirit. We sense the closeness of God in unprecedented ways. We hear prophetic utterances that stir our inner being. We no longer feel ourselves to be mere churchgoers, simply trying to keep the rules of a small, insignificant club which is slightly out of date with the world around it. A fresh longing for revival is in our hearts, prayers are becoming more and more intense, and expectation is more real.

Prepare the way

John the Baptist was sent to make ready a people prepared for the Lord. The last book of the Old Testament sent a warning that the Lord whom we seek would suddenly come to his temple, but who could stand when he appears (Mal 3:1–2)? John the Baptist came to a backslidden generation. He came as a man sent from God. No spokesman for the status quo, he came challenging the system and those who ran it. He quickly gained powerful enemies as he swung his axe with devastating force at the roots of the religious culture. The Pharisees' claims to be the children of

Abraham were dismissed as irrelevant by a man who was looking for fruit, not jargon. Refusing to take any glory for himself, he longed to hear the Bridegroom's voice. As 'best man' he saw it as his chief goal to help the bride make herself ready.

In aiming to prepare a people John cried out that every valley must be lifted up, while potholes of doubt had to be filled in. A generation not used to seeing God move had become formal and cold. Even his godly father Zechariah frustrated the angel Gabriel with total unbelief when promised a son. Zechariah was struck dumb. Unbelief closes your mouth. Undoubtedly devout, he was nevertheless unbelieving and had to wait until after the event before he could communicate. The tragedy of an unbelieving church is that it fails to speak prophetically. It sounds no warning trumpet but merely brings words of explanation after the event. Every unbelieving valley must be lifted. Attitudes which say, 'It could never happen here' must be abandoned. Levels of expectation must be raised.

Similarly mountains had to be brought low, proud obstacles had to be humbled. The Pharisees and priests who had locked up religion and blocked the way to God had to make way for Jesus who told them, 'You do not enter in, nor will you allow others to.' They represented religion but they did not know God, so they effectively obscured the way to any seeker.

Crooked paths had to be straightened. Jesus hated the crookedness of his generation. They strained at gnats and swallowed camels. No foreign speck was allowed to alight on their drinking water. Special ways of removing them were developed. Gentile gnats were to be strained out. Holiness was to be preserved at all costs. Separation from any form of compromise was to be maintained. The tragic thing was that while they were preoccupied with such minutiae they were failing in real issues of morality without a second thought. The poor were being deprived, widows' homes were swallowed up, while they covered their wickedness with religious jargon and ceremony. Though they had the privilege of John the Baptist's warning, a generation that should have been prepared was nevertheless caught napping.

The arrival of Jesus at the synagogue, as recorded in Luke 4 provides an outstanding illustration. The Lord suddenly came to his temple. God came to church! Having read the scroll of Isaiah 61 Jesus earned the general approval of the congregation. They all spoke well of him, recognising him to be Mary and Joseph's boy, but he was not content with their somewhat patronising response. Putting down the scroll, Jesus took his winnowing fork in his hand and began to attack the bigotry and narrow-mindedness which their synagogue represented.

There had never been such a day in that synagogue before. Soon all Judea would feel the impact of his arrival. The unprepared in the nation would be offended by Jesus. Those who failed to humble themselves by responding correctly to John's preparatory ministry could not cope with the Lord of glory when he stepped upon the stage.

Increasing prayer

I believe that revival is coming to our land. Prayer meetings are multiplying and longings are being expressed. But revival is not as straightforward as we would like to think. Often we read about the history of revivals many years after the event – at a safe distance. Closer inspection of the records often reveals that many religious people were offended by genuine revival; when it happened they were not sure if it was genuinely God. As Arthur Wallis pointed out in his masterly classic on revival *In the Day of Thy Power*, it is often 'a sign spoken against'. We need to make sure that we are humbling ourselves and making ourselves ready lest we should be found wanting. Will you recognise God when he comes, or will you be tempted to dismiss the unexpected?

Even John himself was confused for a moment. Weary and lonely in his cell, John began to hear stories about Jesus that confused him. John regarded his own preaching and appeals for holiness as mere water compared with the fire that Jesus would bring, but now strange stories were reaching him. Instead of living an ascetic life Jesus was mixing with sinners and even eating and drinking with them. Some said they saw a prostitute touching him.

John had his own expectations of Christ, and what he was hearing did not fit those at all. John was in the end only 'a *man* sent from God'. He had to contend with his own limitations – the loneliness, the weariness, the delay, his own temperamental weakness. Jesus was already initiating the small beginnings of a great religious revolution. John's disciples had previously been offended by Jesus' disciples who didn't fast or follow the ceremonial handwashing routines or even apparently have much respect for the Sabbath.

In reality Jesus was introducing something absolutely new. God's New Covenant was being inaugurated. Jesus was beginning a process of spiritual emancipation that would amaze the religious people of his day and bring to birth a new spiritual nation in the earth with implications for every tribe and people. John in his prison cell became the meeting place of two great religions. He was the best that the Old Covenant could produce, but Jesus was introducing a New Covenant which he could not grasp and which left him bewildered.

Soon this New Covenant would be offered to the Gentiles and God would begin to take from the nations a people for himself (see Acts 15:4) fulfilling the promise of Hosea 'I will call those who were not my people "my people"' (see Romans 9:25, NASB). This 'international people' will ultimately provoke to jealousy his ancient people Israel, leading to a 'life from the dead' revival among the Jews which will bless the whole world (Rom 11:13–15). The natural branches will be planted back into their own olive tree and God's people be brought together in fullness (Rom 11:24). To that end Paul made much of his ministry among the Gentiles (Rom 11:13) through evangelism and church planting. We must share his vision and goals.

Recently I have been thrilled to hear of tens of thousands of Russian Jews coming to Jesus and being filled with the Holy Spirit. Large churches of both Jews and Gentiles are demonstrating God's victory in Christ. Things are being turned upside down.

Days of enormous upheaval lie ahead for the church of the living God. I believe that much that has been traditionally part of church life will feel fresh shakings and the God who said, 'I will shake all things, that that which cannot be shaken may remain,' will be powerfully at work. He is preparing a bride. He is seeking her from every tribe, tongue and nation and will bring home a glorious people for himself. His church must make herself ready. We must be filled with fresh oil, for the Bridegroom will suddenly appear. We are living in days of extraordinary opportunity to once again drink deeply of the Holy Spirit in order to be energised and do the work God has called us to do.

As C. H. Spurgeon said,

> A country must be strong in internal resources before it can wisely venture on foreign wars. Thus it is in the great battle for truth; a poor, starving church cannot fight the devil and its armies ... so you see that first of all to keep the church happy and holy within herself there must be a manifestation of the power of the Holy Spirit, and secondly, that the Church may invade the territories of the enemy and may conquer the world for Christ, she must be clothed with the same sacred energy ... The one thing I want to say is this; you cannot get out of the Church what is not in it. The reservoir itself must be filled before it can pour out a stream. We must ourselves drink from the living water until we are full and then from us will flow rivers of living water but not until then. (Robert Backhouse (ed.), *Spurgeon on Revival*, Kingsway Publications, 1996)

Let's receive the Spirit, restore the church and reach the nations for Jesus!

NEW FRONTIERS INTERNATIONAL

Terry Virgo and a team of apostles, prophets, evangelists and pastor/teachers currently serve 170 churches in eleven nations. Working together under the title New Frontiers International their goal is to restore the church, make disciples, train leaders, plant churches and reach the nations. In addition to serving local churches they are also involved in the following ministries:

Training Programmes

Several training courses which are designed to prepare people of all ages for a variety of ministries. Details are available from Woodside Christian Centre, Dover Crescent, Bedford, Beds, MK41 8QH, UK.

Conferences

Stoneleigh International Bible Week attracts over 20,000 people each year. Other conferences covering specific groups and ministries are also arranged. Details can be obtained from the Conference Department, New Frontiers International, 17 Clarendon Villas, Hove, East Sussex, BN3 3RE, UK.

Literature

The magazine, *Frontline International*, keeps you up to date with New Frontiers International news and provides teaching articles. We also produce a curriculum for children and young people called *The Feast* and various books, together with ministry and worship tapes and teaching videos. Enquiries to New Frontiers International, 17 Clarendon Villas, Hove, East Sussex, BN3 3RE, UK. E-mail: 100755.2121@compuserve.com. Visit our Web site on:
http://ourworld.compuserve.com/homepages/nfi/